Saving
What
Remains

ALSO BY LIVIA BITTON-JACKSON

SAVING WHAT REMAINS

*A Holocaust Survivor's Journey Home
to Reclaim Her Ancestry*

LIVIA BITTON-JACKSON

THE LYONS PRESS

GUILFORD, CONNECTICUT

An imprint of The Globe Pequot Press

The Lyons Press is an imprint of The Globe Pequot Press.

Interior designer: Sheryl Kober
Layout artist: Kim Burdick

Library of Congress Cataloging-in-Publication Data is available on file.

ISBN 978-1-59921-546-4

Printed in the United States of America

10 9 8 7 6 5 4 3 2 1

To the memory of my mother for initiating the rescue of our past.

CONTENTS

CONTENTS

SAVING
WHAT
REMAINS

CHAPTER ONE

A Hazardous Mission

JULY 1980

THE CAR SPEEDS ALONG THE COASTAL ROAD, THROUGH THE STILL DAWN AND between rows of palms swaying in the Mediterranean breeze. A soft yellow light suffuses the horizon. Sand dunes emerge from the shadows. The sea itself is still plunged in darkness. Only a muted murmur betrays its nearness. The little white Fiat shoots like an arrow to the Jerusalem intersection. Here it makes a sharp left and continues to race past avocado fields and orange groves, toward Ben-Gurion Airport. More than two years have passed since that night, when Mother confided her fervent wish and charged me with a solemn task.

"Don't go yet," she said, placing a fragile hand on my forearm. "I must talk to you."

I was taken aback; it was unusual for Mother to detain me. She had a habit of urging me to cut my visits short, to leave before dark.

"I want to talk to you about something," she said now with uncharacteristic ceremony. My heart stood still as I searched her eyes for a clue. Gripping the polished mahogany arms, I lowered myself back into the chair with the heavy weight of apprehension.

"Yes, Mom?"

Mother drew her frail posture erect, and for a moment I caught a glimpse of the proud beauty she had once been.

"I had a visitor last night from Australia," she began. "Alfred Stern—do you remember him?"

"Alfred Stern?"

"He left Samorin many years ago. His family owned the paper mill in town. Perhaps you remember the paper mill."

I remembered the paper mill very well. As a child I was fascinated by the enormous cutting machines and the huge reams of shiny white paper propped up against the walls.

"Yes, Mom. I remember the paper mill."

"Alfred is visiting relatives in Israel, and he came to see me. He came to Israel via Czechoslovakia, and he stopped off in Samorin." Mother paused, and I waited for her to go on. What was she trying to tell me?

"Alfred brought disturbing news. The Czechoslovak government is planning to build a dam on the Danube, south of Bratislava, not far from Samorin. Once the dam is built, the entire countryside will be flooded. The region alongside the river will be underwater."

"And?"

"The Jewish cemetery is there. It will be flooded. All the graves . . . all the graves will be obliterated, swept away by the waters of the Danube!"

Her voice grew hoarse. "After Alfred left, I could not fall asleep. I thought of my dear parents." Mom never mentioned her parents without the epithet *dear*. "I thought of my dear parents' graves . . . under tons of water. Their remains, swept away by the river . . . who knows where? Who knows where the Danube will dump my dear parents' remains?"

Mother's words trailed off, dissipated into the dark corners. Her erect posture folded like a pack of cards as she intoned slowly, her voice heavy with fatigue: "They are the only graves . . . the only graves we have, and these, too, will be gone. Gone."

She sighed. It was so out of character for her; sadness wrapped itself around her entire being. "The others—my sister, my three brothers, their wives, and their children—were consumed by fire . . . turned to ash in the crematoria of Auschwitz. They drifted to the sky as smoke. And now my dear parents' remains, the only thing left to us, will be destroyed by water . . . swept away by the Danube."

Mother fell silent, and her eyes—half an hour ago, glistening blue steel—were dark pools.

My heart filled with pain. My mother's pain has for years been my pain. We were like one, my mother and I. Ever since our time together in the Nazi death camps, there has been no clear demarcation line between our two selves.

During my childhood and adolescence before the Holocaust, my mother, a great believer in obedience, kept me in line with an admixture of strict discipline and copious love, free of pampering. She was caring and protective but did not believe in "mollycoddling."

"Hugging and kissing will make you even softer than you are. Life is hard, and overly sensitive, poetic souls like you have to be hardened—not made softer. If I took you in my lap you'd never get off," she used to say whenever I pointed out other mothers' ways of coddling and use of endearments. I yearned for coddling and endearments, but Mom would have none of it. She believed she was doing her duty as a mother by preparing me for life.

From the moment of our incarceration, it all changed dramatically; a radical reversal of roles took place. Within weeks Mom had lost a great deal of weight from extreme starvation, and along with her physical weakness, the strength of her spirit ebbed. She lost her will to live, to fight for survival, and it was I, the thirteen-year-old, timid adolescent girl, who stepped into the role of caregiver to my firm, forty-eight-year old parent, and, imperceptibly, into the role of authority. I helped her and egged her on, sometimes dragging her along by force when her weak legs would not carry her.

After she suffered a severe injury to her upper spine, rendering her virtually incapacitated, it became my responsibility to ensure her survival by sometimes hiding her behind lines and at other times propping her up in a standing position for hours during roll call, or by carrying her on my back during forced marches.

In time, she regained some of her spirit and strength, and our roles equalized. We became the best of friends, soul mates. Our symbiosis continued after liberation from the camps, and, while the resumption of a normal lifestyle restored Mom's authority, our friendship has lived on to the point where each of us senses the emotions of the other, experiencing every nuance.

———•———

When she spoke again, Mother's voice reverberated with renewed energy.

"All night long I kept thinking, and thinking. Something has to be done. Something must be done—before it's too late. It was almost morning when I came up with the idea. Exhumation! I want to have my dear parents' remains exhumed and brought here. To have them buried in Jerusalem!"

Somewhere a streetlight turned on and a faint shaft of light streamed into the room. My mother's searching eyes penetrated the distance between us.

"Elli, what do you think?"

"I . . . I don't know. It sounds fantastic. I don't know . . ." I hesitated.

"Elli, I thought—I hoped you'd agree to do it. Please, think about it. I know if you made up your mind, you could do it," she pleaded.

I could not bear the vulnerable look in Mom's eyes.

"I just don't know. I've never heard of anyone digging up bones from a cemetery in a distant part of the world and shipping them across countries . . . over the ocean."

"It doesn't mean it cannot be done," she said, her voice taking on an argumentative tone.

"Okay, Mom, I'll look into this matter first thing tomorrow," I promised, and bent down to plant a kiss on her deeply furrowed face.

———— ◆ ————

More than two years of red tape ticking through international channels has finally yielded the crucial document from Prague. Sporting a fancy governmental seal—a brilliant red star above the hammer-and-sickle emblem—the permit for the exhumation of Mom's beloved parents is the passport to our mission. With that permit now safely tucked in my handbag, my husband Len and I are heading for Ben-Gurion Airport to catch an El Al flight for Vienna, the first stop on our journey to the realm behind the Iron Curtain.

CHAPTER TWO

On the Way to Europe

CREAM-COLORED CLOUDS DRIFT IN THE AZURE SKY. CLOUDS IN JULY? I HAVE never seen clouds here this time of year. Perhaps late in August, but never in July! This year the sun has been especially relentless throughout the month. Even now at dawn, I can feel the sizzling breath of July rise menacingly from the ground.

Was it a foolish impulse to undertake this mission? Was I being too reckless in going back to my birthplace? My friends' warnings keep echoing in my ears: "What you are about to do is suicidal," said one. "You will be thrown in prison, and disappear without a trace. It has happened to many others," said another. "Let someone else go in your place. Someone without your incriminating record in Czechoslovakia," warned a third, a fellow dissident.

On a bitter cold winter night, thirty-one years ago, I had fled from Czechoslovakia. The illegal escape route led through frozen forests shimmering in moonlight across the border, across the Iron Curtain, to the American Zone in Vienna. When the Party was apprised of my flight, I was declared a "dissident"—a political criminal in Stalinist Czechoslovakia—and sentenced *in absentia* to a twenty-year prison term.

Now Czechoslovakia is still in the throes of a Stalinist-Communist regime. And my criminal conviction still stands.

"You must not go to Czechoslovakia. Such records are retained forever," advised an acquaintance in the diplomatic service. "For you this is an extremely hazardous undertaking."

But there is no choice. I alone know the exact location of the graves. Those graves have been part of my inner world. As a child I used to accompany my mother when she went to pray at her parents' graveside. On the ominous morning of deportation to Auschwitz, the two of us, Mother and I, slipped through the military police cordon and sneaked out to that cemetery to say a final prayer at those two graves—a final good-bye. And when we, skeletal survivors of the death camps, returned to the ruins of our past, our first journey brought us to that graveyard. We found the inscriptions on the graves badly eroded, and to Mom's great delight, I offered to repaint them. I purchased a can of gold paint for my grandmother's black granite tomb, and a can of black paint for my grandfather's gray marble one. Balancing a borrowed ladder on the back of a borrowed bicycle, I rode the six kilometers to the cemetery, climbed on top of the ladder to reach all parts of the massive monuments, and painstakingly repainted every letter of the inscriptions.

There is no other alternative. I am the one to go.

Bubi, my brother, also believed I was doing a reckless thing, but did not try to stop me. And Mother, who has always fretted about my every move, no matter how innocuous, now said: "You are embarking on a holy mission. God will be with you."

My husband Len, bless his romantic Irish heart, has taken a leave from the clinic in Israel where he works as a physician. He's packed his bag, saying simply: "I am going with you. Just in case. To get you out of prison."

———◆———

Ben-Gurion Airport is alive with activity. The familiar large, blue-lettered poster wooing tourists—COME BACK SOON! WE MISS YOU

7

ALREADY!—now seems to convey an ominous message. I shudder: Will I come back?

As if sensing my panic, Len's fingers fold about my hand. "Not to worry, darling. Everything will work out fine."

Check-in and seat selection are swift. Len and I do not get seats next to each other. There are no adjacent seats even in the smoking section. My seat is on the other side of the aisle from Len's, one row behind.

After he buckles in, Len turns and calls out a cheery, encouraging "Bon Voyage." I force a smile, buckle my seat belt, and prepare to sink into a sea of thoughts. But a gray-haired woman and her thin-featured husband on my right introduce themselves and eagerly confide that this would be their first trip abroad ever since they had come to Israel fifty years ago, he from Poland, she from Germany. The couple's infectious excitement and enthusiastic conversation dissipate my thoughts. Listening to their friendly chatter, I watch the magnificent Mediterranean shimmer below. Soon the sea is replaced by stretches of dark forest and a string of snowcapped hills. My companions exclaim, "How beautiful!" and ask which country we have just passed over. I am not sure whether it is northern Italy or Yugoslavia. My hesitant guess passes for information and the couple eagerly forwards it to a young man right behind them. They had met him at Ben-Gurion Airport, and he'd told them he had just been discharged from the army and was doing what many young Israelis in his position do: using his army pay for a tour abroad. This was his very first trip out of Israel.

"But I'm not sure," I warn. "We must ask the stewardess." I do not want the young Israeli to start his great encounter with the world misinformed.

Just then, the intercom announces that we are flying above Yugoslavia.

I lean back and close my eyes. I remember the thrill of my first flight. How long ago was it? How many times have I flown since then? Across how many oceans, each flight the promise of a new adventure . . .

But none of those flights had reached Central Europe. I had vowed never to go back there. And now, to fulfill my mother's wish, I am going back. More than three decades later, I am returning to Czechoslovakia, to the little town near the Danube that has so long lived in my anguished memory. And where I am risking arrest upon arrival.

Once, I was happy in that little town near the Danube. I had lived there with Father, Mother, Bubi, and some chickens and geese in a sprawling yellow house flanked by acacia trees, a five-minute bike ride from the house and the lilac garden of Aunt Serena, my favorite aunt.

My father, Mark, a tall, lean, silent man possessed of the wisdom of resignation, and my mother, Laura, a strong-willed woman filled with a robust zest for life, tended our general store, which dominated the entire house front on Main Street. My older brother, Bubi, a blond, gangly boy with ready humor, forever teased me and played tricks on me when he wasn't in school, on the junior soccer field, or involved in a game of cops-and-robbers with the neighborhood children. I, a gawky girl with long blond braids, watched the boys yearningly as they played around the hill on the southern end of the house, and dreamt of the day when they would allow me to join in their game. Mother's widowed older sister, soft-spoken Aunt Serena, sewed dresses for me and showered me with a thousand other tokens of her affection.

I believed the pastoral tranquility of our lives would last forever. I believed we would always live in the yellow corner house flanked by acacia trees.

Then, suddenly, the rumble of tanks and the cadence of goose-steps shattered the serenity of that world. First they took away the store. Then they "requisitioned" the merchandise, placed a seal on the store entrance, and stamped the house with a huge yellow "Jewish" star. The inhabitants of the corner house were marked. For what? We did not know.

On a sunny spring day in 1944 we found out. My mother, my father, my aunt, my brother and I, together with the five hundred and sixteen other Jews of our little town, were herded to the train station and locked into cattle cars destined for Auschwitz.

————◆————

"Ladies and gentlemen, we have landed at Vienna Airport. We hope you have had a pleasant flight. Please refrain from smoking and remain in your seats until the plane comes to a standstill."

I'm back. God help me.

The middle-aged couple and the young soldier bid an excited farewell. Len reaches for the hand luggage in the overhead bin.

"How was your flight, darling?"

"Okay."

"Mine, too. I read most of the time."

"Len . . ."

"Yes?"

"Nothing."

"Are you all right? You look pale. Are you all right?"

"I'm fine, thank you—really," I whisper, with eyes downcast and a quivering voice. Len, unconvinced, casts worried glances in my direction.

The airbus stops in front of the terminal in the heart of the city near the Donaukanal. Vienna is bathed in the noontide sun. The poplars beyond the canal jubilate in dazzling green.

"Len, look," I exclaim. "The bright green trees, on the other side of the Danube Canal—that must be the Stadtpark, the city park of Vienna. Do you hear music? Of course! It's Sunday. The open-air orchestra is playing in the park . . . the Sunday concert in the park!"

Just like then, many years ago . . . Amazing—there's still a Sunday concert in the Stadtpark!

"I can hear it distinctly," Len says. "It's Strauss. The Viennese waltz. How appropriate!"

"Would you like to go to the park, find a bench under a tree, and listen to the music—just for a little while?" I ask.

"Why not? It's a marvelous idea. We'll have plenty of time to hunt for a hotel afterwards." Len's face lights up as usual with the anticipation of adventure. I am glad. I want Len to like Vienna. I want him to be happy in Vienna. Len's happiness is my shield against the past—and against the fear of what I am about to undertake.

Len slips his arm into mine and we walk across the bridge. As we walk together in rhythmic, even strides, our belts trailing in the wind, I am no longer afraid.

We find a stone bench near the small lake. I close my eyes and let the breeze wash waves of Strauss over me. Len takes my hand, and suddenly, inexplicably, the fragrance of water lilies wafts into my innermost world.

CHAPTER THREE

ARI

MAY, 1949

STRAINS OF STRAUSS MINGLE WITH THE SCENT OF WATER LILIES. BUT ARI'S insistent voice keeps intruding on the music: "Are you coming with me to Palestine? Are you joining the transport? Are you? Give me your answer, Elli. Give me your answer now."

His grip on my fingers is a steel clamp."Give me an answer, Elli."

The sound of music, the fragrance of water lilies, and Ari's relentless claim blend with the storm in my soul.

"The transport is leaving in a few days, perhaps a week. You must come with me. You belong with us, in Palestine . . . in Eretz Yisrael. You'll not be happy anywhere else."

I taste a salty trickle on my lips.

"Please don't cry."

The trickle turns into a thin steady stream. Why can't I be like the others? Why can't I just join the transport with Ari and the gang? I love him, and I love the gang. And I yearn to go to Eretz Yisrael. Is the promise I had given Mother, that we'd follow my brother to America, the only reason? Isn't my weakness the true reason . . . the fact that I'm not able to part from my mother, and my brother . . . Isn't that why I'm unable to make the choice?

"Please, stop crying." Ari's timid arm about my shoulders does not bring any comfort.

No one in the gang understands my agony. Not one of them has relatives, attachments. Auschwitz canceled all attachments, they say bitterly. We have no attachments, connections, no debts, no dilemmas. We owe nothing, we expect nothing.

I do not have that gift. I do have attachments, thank God . . . But now my attachments are weeping wounds.

Ari's trembling touch is the caress of despair:"Please stop crying."

They will leave soon, the transport. Canvas-covered trucks through Yugoslavia, Italy . . . the Haganah boats across the Mediterranean to the shores of Palestine. Soon they'll be gone.Will I ever see them again?

"Let's get back to the camp,"Ari says. "It's getting late."

It is dusk by the time we reach the Rothschild Hospital. The wards and hallways of this rambling structure are home for hundreds of refugees, Jews from Poland, Czechoslovakia, Hungary, and Romania. It is a transit camp.We are in transit for the hope of a better future.

Ari's twin brother, Tuvia, greets us with the news. Registration for the transport has already begun!

Tuvia misunderstands Ari's lack of response. "Don't worry," he says cheerfully, "we'll make the list. The Haganah needs cannon fodder. There's renewed fighting with the Arabs. Don't you fret, brother, we'll make the list."

Ari climbs the stairs without speaking. Tuvia turns to me:"What's eating him?"

I follow Ari up the stairs.

"Why the long faces? I thought he'd start dancing the hora when he heard the news. And look at him now. The idealist. The thought of a little fighting gives him cold feet. Ari, it's your dream come true.You told us to love the Land, if need be, with a spade—if need be, with a gun.Your very own words, Ari."

We reach the end of the corridor. The desk of the Palestinian delegate is mobbed.We join the end of the line. By the time the brothers' turn comes, the list is almost full. Ari and Tuvia are among the last, the other members of the gang having registered earlier.They all made it to the transport.

Except me.

I make my way to our room. "Where have you been?"Mother greets me, her face aflame with anxiety. "You were out all afternoon, and no one knew where you were. You said you were going for a walk with one of the boys, but that was five hours ago. What happened?"

I tell Mom of the transport. And of Ari's proposal of marriage. Mother does not answer. Silently she arranges plates on the narrow school desk that serves as our dining room table.

"Let's eat," she says finally, and we maneuver our bodies in between the low desk and the narrow bench attached to it on both sides. "The food is getting cold. I've been waiting for you a long time."

Twenty-two other people share our hospital ward that is bedroom, living room, dining room, and kitchen for all of us. Army blankets hung on strings separate the living quarters.

The gang lives in another ward, but they are daily visitors, and all the occupants of my ward know them and tease me about them. They have nicknames for each. Ari is the idealist, Tuvia the sport, Peter the playboy, Elie the athlete, Leizer the gentleman, Hayim the tough guy, and Leslie, the scholar. They like Ari the best and place bets on our romance.

"Don't cry. Eat your soup," Mother says. "If you want to go to Palestine so badly, we'll talk about it. There will be other transports. We'll find a way."

Mother is making a valiant effort, I know. This makes me even more miserable.

The next day, the transport gathers in the hospital yard. One by one, the boys take their leave. Hayim presses his fountain pen in my hand. "It's yours," he says with a wink. "Write beautiful poems with it, and send me copies."

Elie hands me a bouquet of lilies: "Your favorite." His handshake is firm. "Hazak," he says in Hebrew. "Hazak v'amatz. Be strong and take courage."

"Hazak v'amatz," I mumble, and swallow hard. Leizer has his favorite book of poetry in his hands. Is he going to read Ady, the Hungarian poet he idolizes, on the truck across the Austrian-Italian hills, or aboard the refugee vessel to Haifa port?

Leizer hands me the book with an embarrassed smile: "I want you to keep this . . . until you come to Eretz Yisrael. Bring it with you. Okay?" Also Leslie, Peter, and Tuvia have parting gifts, parting words. Ari is last. Ari averts his eyes as he shakes my hand, then without a word turns and makes a run for the truck.

"Ari!" My heart is stuck in my throat. Without turning back, Ari hops on the truck and disappears between the canvas flaps of the opening. Through a haze of tears I see the others wave before disappearing in the covered army vehicle. The convoy of trucks moves out of the yard. The cloud of exhaust fumes and the distant rumbling of the departing trucks seem like the echo of a lost dream. Like a sleepwalker I return to camp, clutching the flowers and my souvenirs.

The gang is gone. No more picnics in the forest behind the camp. No more expeditions to the Stadtpark to hear the open-air orchestra. No more trips to the Schoenbrunn . . . to the Burg. They are gone, and I am to face Vienna without them.

I am to face life without them.

Mom puts the flowers in a glass of water, and the large room fills with the overpowering fragrance of water lilies.

CHAPTER FOUR

Vienna

THE GOLDENE SPINNE IS A SMALL HOTEL NEAR THE STADTPARK WHERE THE beds are of imperial size, the bathtub has the shape of an oyster, and the windows open to a panorama of Gothic spires etched against the Austrian Alps.

We unpack quickly and go for a stroll on the Ring. As we turn into Kaertnerstrasse, I am stunned by unanticipated change. The crowded business street I remembered is transformed into a spacious pedestrian mall where tourists in a brilliant array of costumes sit at tables under colorful umbrellas. European dress intermingles with Indian saris, African togas, and American blue jeans. The variety of languages is just as striking: We hear German, English, French, Swahili, Hindustani, and Arabic. This is a new Vienna, this kaleidoscope of cultures and races. We are encountering the gate of a new Europe.

It is quite a feat to find two empty seats. The other occupants of the table are a young French couple and three women who converse in a combination of Spanish and Italian. Len and I are soon chatting with them all, inserting English into the admixture of languages.

All at once, glancing at his watch, Len exclaims: "It's way past midnight! We have a busy day tomorrow."

We apologize for our hasty departure, and set out for the Goldene Spinne on foot.

The down covers on the large beds are a godsend. They smother the sudden chill of the night and my apprehension of tomorrow.

"Good morning!"

I bury my face in the pillow and do not respond.

"There's no time to snooze," Len calls crisply. "We're behind schedule. Remember the Czechoslovak Embassy? We were planning to be there by eight o'clock."

"What time is it?"

"Eight o'clock."

"My God!"

I dress in a fury. We have to get Len's Czechoslovak visa today. We could not apply for it at home. Czechoslovakia has no diplomatic relations with Israel. I had obtained mine in Washington with the help of a friend in the civil service. How could I have overslept, today of all days?

I tuck a bundle of papers into my handbag. To play it safe I'd brought along every document in our possession—identity cards, marriage and birth certificates, permits of every size and color.

Except our Israeli passports. Mr. Bloch, the hotel manager, kindly agrees to keep these "incriminating" credentials in the hotel's safe during our stay in Czechoslovakia. He understands that we intend to cross behind the Iron Curtain with our American passports. The Czechoslovak authorities must not know that we are from Israel.

At breakfast I buttered some rolls and tucked them into my bag: The day at the Czechoslovak Embassy might prove to be long and grueling.

A savage wet wind plasters the red-white-and-blue flag high above the entrance against the facade of the embassy building. The familiar colors of my native land now fill me with dread.

The stairwell leads into a large lobby filled with dense human vapor. Within seconds, Len and I are submerged in the mass of people that fills the hall to capacity. Who is in charge here? To whom can one turn for information? My attempts to glean knowledge from the people around us are an instant failure. In the frantic crowd no one knows what is to be done.

After a while, two rows of anxious bodies form from the throng, each pressing toward a small window at one end of the room. Heavy metal bars crisscross the narrow aperture, behind which is the stolid figure of an official in a Soviet-style uniform. At long last, in a far corner of the room, we discover a table piled high with various application blanks. We snatch one and fill it out, while joining one of the two lines at random, beginning a slow, agonizing advance toward the window.

Three hours later we reach the window, and Len slides the completed application forms together with snapshots and his Canadian passport under the heavy metal bars. The stony-faced, uniformed official promptly shoves the papers back under the bars.

"Next!" he barks in the harsh dialect of Upper Slovakia, motioning for the papers of the next applicant.

"What's wrong?" Len asks, startled. I translate, but the official ignores the question. "Move on," he barks without looking at us. "You're blocking the traffic."

"What's wrong?" I repeat in Slovak, uncomprehending. But the next applicant elbows Len aside in his anxiety to reach the window.

"I don't know," I say to Len; we are both baffled. "He wouldn't answer my question."

What has happened? Was this an arbitrary rejection of Len's visa? And if so, why? Is it the end of the line for us, or should I carry on without Len? "After all, I do have a visa," I say.

"It's out of the question," Len protests. "You cannot take the chance to go alone; it's too risky. You cannot go without me."

There is no other official around, no one to turn to for clarification. There is only a mass of applicants crashing forward with single-minded determination. In a desperate, last-ditch effort I turn with my question to the young uniformed guard at the entrance. To our surprise, the young guard gives a cordial answer. He explains that the snapshots have to be glued to the first page of the application forms!

Was that all? Len and I look at each other, dumbfounded, our sense of relief palpable.

"Where can one get glue around here?" I venture, and the young guard directs me to a table where an assertive crowd of applicants is battling over a jar of glue.

The second time around, the grim Slovak official accepts the forms without comment and in return thrusts a yellow slip of paper under the bars. A number scribbled on the yellow slip indicates our turn.

An hour later the granite-faced bureaucrat barks out Len's number, and when I make my way to the window, he shoves Len's Canadian passport under the bars. I open it slowly, my hands trembling, and find the appropriate page. There, in the middle of the page, is stamped the Czechoslovak visa with the familiar emblem!

All at once, a sudden commotion draws everyone's attention. At the window stands a white-robed Arab shaking his fist menacingly and unleashing a colorful flow of invective in classical Arabic at the Communist official behind the bars.

"No picture! No picture!" he bellows now in English, and angrily yanks a veiled figure in front of the window. "See: Here she is! She is my wife! No picture!"

The Slovak official is unperturbed. Without moving so much as a facial muscle, he announces, with finality: "Picture."

The Arab shakes a clenched fist: "No picture!"

"Picture!" The Arab's documents are flying in all directions from the sheer force of the thrust from behind the bars. The Arab, without losing his composure, first leans close to the bars, and then moves a step backwards, making a sudden forward motion with his head. The next instant, a splash of spittle hangs above the official's right eye. For a moment, the rock-like face staggers backward. A second later a terrible roar thunders from behind the bars: "Your passport!"

A triumphant sneer lights up the Arab's face. With a gesture of utter condescension he flips his passport under the bars. There is hushed silence in the room. The crowd watches with bated breath as the embassy official ceremoniously opens the book to the page where the Arab's visa has been stamped. With slow, deliberate motion, he lifts a seal and lets it slam with enormous force onto the page. When the embassy official raises his hand again, right across the Czechoslovak visa, the word CANCELED is stamped in red ink.

"Here!" The official's voice cuts like steel. "You will never enter Czechoslovakia!" He looks the Arab square in the face for the first time. "Never!"

The Arab's hand trembles violently as he reaches for his passport. He grips his veiled wife by the arm and storms out of the hall, dragging her along like a rag doll. Then the embassy official pulls a white handkerchief from his pocket, slowly wipes the spittle from above his right eye, and reaches for the documents of the next applicant. In a few minutes, the stunned silence in the room rises to a din of organized chaos, and the former hubbub, the business-as-usual frenzy, quickly resumes.

The incident leaves me deeply perturbed, and for some time I forget my own predicament. I keep thinking of that unfortunate Arab woman, totally bereft of autonomy, of personhood . . . even of self.

What does the future hold for her? How will she, if ever, throw off the chains of her repression?

When we leave the embassy, the realization slowly sinks in: We have received the visa for Len to enter Czechoslovakia! However, the full force of relief sweeps over me only when Len and I sit in a pub near the embassy, with two mugs of beer between us. The full-bodied Czech beer courses through my tension and dissolves it.

For the moment, my fear is gone.

CHAPTER FIVE

Crossing the Iron Curtain

NOW IT IS TEN MINUTES PAST TWO AND OUR BUS IS NOWHERE TO BE SEEN. At two o'clock it was to leave for Bratislava from Vienna's main terminal. For more than an hour, Len and I have been waiting on the platform in the midst of a large crowd.

Finally, at two twenty-five, a dark green, somewhat battle-worn bus pulls up to the curb, and its doors slide open with a pitiful screech. Instantly, a handful of passengers separate from the crowd, and a listless, thin line starts a reluctant ascent into the vehicle.

Many more people remain on the platform. They surround the bus, waving frantically and shouting tearful words of farewell. Lips are pressed against the windowpanes. Kisses are smudged on either side of the polished glass. Desperate cries of *Viszontlátásra! Dovidenia! Auf Wiedersehen!*—"See you again," in Hungarian, Slovak, and German.

These are no casual partings. The passengers that board the bus are no casual visitors. They are close family members who had been deprived of all contact for years, and now, after a brief reunion, are bidding farewell . . . until the next time. When would that be? In how many years, if ever? Vienna and Bratislava are separated only by thirty kilometers, and yet they are worlds apart. One belongs to the West, and the other, to the Communist Bloc. They are two worlds divided by the Iron Curtain.

Len and I also board the ramshackle bus and take two seats at the rear. From here through the window, we watch the spectacle of the tearful, gesticulating crowd, and witness the drama and anguish of leave-taking, manifestations of concern for their loved ones, for the danger they face in crossing the border.

All at once, I feel forlorn watching the sea of waving arms, with not a single gesture of farewell meant for us . . . If only one pair of eyes would send a smile of encouragement. This journey holds no less anxiety for us. For us, this border crossing holds perhaps even greater peril.

The doors close and the bus begins to move, then gathers speed, leaving the grief-stricken crowd behind. With a sharp turn, it leaves the terminal and slips into heavy commercial traffic. Soon we cross the Danube Canal and leave the Austrian capital behind. The bus rolls out onto the open highway and the traffic thins. We ease quite imperceptibly into the familiar realm of rolling green countryside studded by barnyards, grain silos, and an occasional haystack.

Isolated Swabian villages, small clusters of farmsteads centered about white church steeples, make an appearance on the roadside. Then even these recede into the distance and give free play to stretches of open fields. For endless kilometers, you can see nothing but telephone poles spinning in the dust.

A young Dutch tourist engages Len in a conversation about his recent trip to Czechoslovakia.

"The country is like a huge prison," he intones in a loud voice. "People walk around listlessly, in drab clothes, always looking over their shoulders. They behave as if they were expecting to be arrested or gunned down at any moment. Wait till you see the machine guns," he says, "as soon as we approach the Czechoslovak border. It's frightening. The whole country is frightening."

I cannot believe my ears. Is this young Dutch fellow out of his mind? How dare he speak so openly and so loudly in a Czechoslovak bus? Is he high on drugs? Is he drunk?

"Please, make no comment. Try to ignore him," I say to Len in an undertone.

But the young man is not easy to ignore. He insists on continuing his reckless harangue. He has visited all the Communist Bloc countries, he boasts, and deplores the mess they are in.

"What a farce!" he exclaims with a sarcastic chuckle. "You know, I used to be a Communist. My friends and I believed in Communism. That's why we went behind the Iron Curtain, on a holy pilgrimage, so to speak. Czechoslovakia, Hungary, Poland, Yugoslavia. What a joke. A gulag world, all of them! You should see the breadlines in Poland!"

We cannot risk listening to this. Somehow, I have to shut him up. Without waiting for an opening, I cut into his harangue with stories of our visit to his native country. Len joins in, and together we recount to him our amusing mishaps on a boat in the Amsterdam canal.

The young Dutchman humors us by listening to our stories, but only briefly. During a momentary lull in the conversation, he is back again with renewed fury, bitterly disparaging his fallen idol, the "Communist entity," as he calls it. I am beginning to panic. What can I do to shut him up?

All of the sudden, the bus stops with a jolt, and the long line of traffic comes to a standstill.

"We are approaching the border," our young companion explains. "It's a slow process. First comes the Austrian, then, after a long gap, the Czech border outpost. They all take their time. Especially the Czechs. Might as well take a nap," he announces unexpectedly, and leans back in his seat with his eyes closed. What a relief!

An Austrian officer in a gray uniform boards the bus.

"Attention, please," he announces in German. "Prepare your passports for inspection." The officer passes down the aisle, and Len hands him our passports. After a brief glance he returns our documents without comment, continuing his inspection. Once it is completed, the Austrian officer gives a smart salute and leaves the bus. The bus begins to move, and together with a long line of traffic, passes through the raised barrier of the Austrian border.

Five hundred meters down the road the bus comes to a halt again. The doors fling open, and another uniformed figure enters. The sight of this dreaded forest-green uniform, with its high red collar and epaulets trimmed with red stars, contracts my stomach into a tennis ball. Stiffly, without introduction, the Communist officer moves down the aisle, and in deadly silence, collects all the passports.

I hold my breath as he grimly snatches our passports from Len's hand and adds them to the pile in his hand. Then, without uttering a sound, he leaves the bus, taking the pile of passports with him. Not one of the passengers moves.

Half an hour passes in a tense, silent vigil. What is going on? What's taking so long? What has happened to the passports? Why is everyone silent? Something must be terribly wrong. Dread is creeping into my bowels.

Another fifteen minutes pass. The bus begins to roll.

"Where are they taking us without our passports?" I whisper my panic in Len's ear. "Where are our passports?" My stomach, the tiny tennis ball, is now blocking my windpipe. I have difficulty breathing.

"Don't worry," Len says. "You're not the only one whose passport has been detained."

"But I'm not like everyone else," I manage to say.

"Please, relax," Len pleads. "There's nothing to worry about. This is routine passport control."

From my seat on the bus, I can see the tall watchtower with the machine gun–toting guard the Dutch tourist had mentioned. Cold sweat trickles down my spine.

I am convinced that it's my papers that are causing the delay! At this precise moment, my papers are being investigated, and telephone calls are crisscrossing between Prague and Bratislava. Soon, very soon, my background will be discovered. I will be arrested and held incommunicado. Just like the young Hungarian boy who disappeared from the Russian Zone in Vienna, and was never heard from again. Like several members of the Haganah transport I had helped organize, and like the two sisters from Rumania who vanished forever from this very border . . . just one night before Mom and I made it across.

I close my eyes to quiet the throbbing in my temples, and to shut out the sight of the sentry with the enormous machine gun in the watchtower.

CHAPTER SIX

The Escape

FEBRUARY 1949

THE MACHINE GUNS ARE SILENT NOW. SILENCE LIKE A FROZEN BLANKET ENVELOPS the white, shimmering forest. The truck's engine and headlights are shut off, and the camouflaged vehicle is a phantom floating soundlessly among the trees. Our driver's uncanny ability to navigate the woods from Bratislava through the Russian Zone to Vienna in total darkness is the key to this secret escape route. His record is the best among the drivers of the Haganah convoys; he has made this run many times, and not once has his truck been detected.

Tonight there's faint moonlight. That's dangerous. The Russian guards are very alert. Although the Slovak border police are heavily bribed, one must be wary of them, too. Last week they opened fire on a Haganah convoy after it passed their guidepost. Two women and a child from Poland were killed. And yesterday, the Rausnitz sisters from Rumania, together with their guide . . .

Mother and I huddle close together. Her face and hands are as cold as ice. All of a sudden there is a burst of machine-gun fire somewhere in the distance. Thank goodness, we are beyond its range! The truck moves much faster now, and then, after an interminable gap of total silence, the ignition and headlights are turned on. All the passengers on the bus burst into spontaneous applause.

"Hush—haverim," the driver warns. "Not yet . . . not yet. We're not out of danger yet." But I can tell there is relief in his voice. Mom and I embrace, and I smother her face with kisses. We are both weeping now, silently, our hearts burdened with happiness. The vehicle goes fast now, and soon we are on the open road. I take a peek through a gap in the canvas near our seat. It is quiet out there. No machine-gun fire. The dark forest is looming far behind us.

We have made it.

CHAPTER SEVEN

The Bridge

J*UST BEYOND THE WATCHTOWER WITH THE GUN-TOTING GUARDS, THE BUS* comes to a halt. A sudden loud clatter breaks the frozen silence in the vehicle as the doors fling open. In the entrance, a uniformed figure appears and snaps an order in rapid Slovak: "Everyone off the bus. Take all your things."

The passengers who understand Slovak anxiously collect their belongings and scamper off the bus. The others, in bewildered confusion, inquire from each other: "What did he say?"

"Everyone must leave the bus," I volunteer. "With their luggage." Within minutes the bus is empty of passengers. The young Dutchman shrugs his shoulders and sullenly drags his backpack off the bus. Len lunges ahead, carrying the larger suitcase. His unbuttoned raincoat flutters in a gust of wind as he dashes across an open, pebble-strewn square toward a low, barrack-like building.

"Len, wait for me," I call after him, breathless with the effort to keep up.

"Darling, you look ghastly. Are you all right?" Len puts down the suitcase. "Let me help you. Give me your valise."

"I . . . I'm fine. Just a bit faint. It'll pass."

In the building, at the end of a long corridor, we find a bench where I stop to rest while Len proceeds to the inspection hall with our luggage. A while later, I follow Len to the huge depot, bustling with activity. Long counters are laden with empty valises and heaps of personal items. Passengers fiddle nervously with zippers and locks, flinging open lids of luggage in an exaggerated show of cooperation. And the inspectors, sensing their victims' vulnerability, wield gruffness as a badge of authority.

I find Len nonchalantly leaning against our luggage, patiently awaiting his turn. As I approach, his face lights up.

"Ah, here you are! How's it going? Did you get a bit of rest?"

"Yes, thank you. I feel much better."

It is our turn. The inspector signals to us to open our luggage, but before we have a chance to comply, he makes an unexpected, expansive gesture with his hand and sends the suitcases sliding along the smooth surface of the counter. He makes a few brief notations on his clipboard, and our inspection is over. We are free to return to the bus! Len flashes me an encouraging you-see-all's-well glance, and we hurry out of the hall.

Gradually the bus fills with passengers. The grim passport inspector enters and hands out the passports without comment. As I hold my American passport in my hand, my nausea is gone and the throbbing in my temples has subsided. The crisis is over—for the moment. The bus rolls past the open barrier and picks up speed.

All at once the Danube comes into view. The Danube. My river. My beautiful river!

"Do you see that bridge?" The young Dutchman points to a remarkable structure rising above the river. "That's a new bridge over the Danube River, built recently," he explains. "It's very interesting— a suspension bridge with only one column supporting it at one end. Can you see the circular structure way up on top?" he continues. "It's a café, built on an incredibly high column. There's a pretty view from way up there."

Now the bus is ascending the ramp onto the new bridge. Below, the Danube flows lazily, like molten lead. Mighty, unhurried, it flows with familiar dignity and indifference.

The bridge affords an extraordinary panorama, a view from a totally new vantage point. I have never seen the Danube from this angle. From here, I can see the entire range of mountains beyond the river to the north, and, turning my head to the south, I can see the spot where the river splits into two branches to enclose a green island. In the lush woods of that island, about eighteen kilometers from here, nestles the small town where I was born.

"Look at the Danube, Len. Isn't it beautiful?"

"But I've always thought of it as the Blue Danube," says Len. "It's not blue at all. It's gray, just like any other river."

"Because the sky's overcast. The Danube mirrors the sky. When the sky is clear, the Danube is blue."

"I suppose," Len allows, not quite convinced.

The Dutch tourist gives a knowing smile. "There are no blue rivers anymore. They are all polluted. All the rivers of the world are filthy and gray, and the Danube is no exception."

I know better. The Danube is different. The Danube always mirrors the sky. When the sky is unclouded and bright, the Danube is clear blue with millions of silvery ripples on its surface . . .

CHAPTER EIGHT

The Danube

JULY 1943

"*TODAY THE RIPPLES ON THE SURFACE OF THE RIVER LOOK EVEN MORE BRILLIANT then usual!*" I cry with excitement.

"Perhaps because it's late afternoon. It has something to do with the angle of the sun," Papa explains.

"Papa, can I go in for one more swim?" Bubi pleads. "It's not even four yet. Just one more swim?"

"Enough swimming for one day." Papa's voice is heavy with a suppressed sigh. "We must go home."

I know how badly my brother wants just one more swim, and it makes me sad. Golden sunshine breaks through the foliage and dapples the shade. Here in the woods it is cool despite the summer heat. Insects cavort and hum in the shaft of light, and lend a soft accompaniment to the deep murmur of the river.

"It's God's gift, this perfect harmony," Papa sighs, and rises from the blanket. "Balm to the soul."

"Who knows when we'll come again?" I say. "Papa, you yourself said . . . Papa, please let Bubi go in for just one more swim."

Papa's smile is indulgent yet very sad. "Okay. One more swim. You can go too. But be quick about it—and dry yourselves fast."

Shrieking, Bubi and I dash into the crystal-clear ripples. I wince with the impact of the cold water but cannot linger over my discomfort. Bubi is nearing the tall white rock, his starting point. My starting point is the little embankment, far below. Bubi gives me a head start.

I swim with all my might, but soon I hear my brother approaching and splashing past me with an ease I know I will never match. Not in a million years.

Out of breath, I reach the willow, our goal, about a hundred meters downstream. I grasp the overhanging branch and pull myself up the slope. Bubi is waiting. He stands tall and thin and wet, his shoulders slightly stooped, his teeth chattering from the sudden chill.

"Hurry! Run——faster! It's freezing."

"Wait for me! Wait for me!" I can never catch up.

Mom is waiting with the towels. She wraps them around us, pins up my braids. In the distance the herdsman's gong sounds, followed by the rumbling of the cattle and the yelping of the dogs. The approach of the herd marks the end of the summer day.

"Quick," Mother says. "Let's pack our things. The herd will reach us soon, and with them, the mosquitoes. Let's leave a wide margin between us and the herd."

We fold the blankets and Father ties the bundles to the back of his bicycle. By the time we emerge from our forest retreat, the herd is in full view on the wide-open green. We have to make it to the embankment. Beyond the embankment, we are safe from the stench and the swarms of mosquitoes. The sun is setting behind the Carpathian foothills, and darkness is beginning to seep through the warm summer atmosphere when we reach the first houses of the town. Will we ever see the Danube again? This is the summer of 1943, and we sense——we know——that days like these are numbered.

CHAPTER NINE

Bratislava

BEFORE THE BUS ROLLS OFF THE BRIDGE AND SLIPS INTO A TUNNEL, *I* CAST A final, longing glance at my beloved river. I hope that during our stay here I will have a chance to see it up close. I must.

Emerging from the tunnel, the vehicle rolls into a rather shabby neighborhood, snaking through narrow streets, barely clearing the corners of antiquated buildings. The mighty river is far behind us now. The discordant din of ships echoes in the distance while the bus moves on and on amid gray, unfamiliar buildings studded with lifeless windows, austere entrances. Dreariness and dissolution engulfs the city. Is this Bratislava?

Not a single familiar sight, not one remembered landmark, welcomes my searching memory. All is alien. Unremarkable. The bus turns from one dilapidated street into another. The city keeps shrinking into insignificance.

"Soon we'll reach the medieval quarter, called Old Pressburg," I promise Len. "Then you'll see the real Bratislava."

The next sharp turn of the bus presents a shocking surprise: The medieval quarter is gone. Gone . . . replaced by a "modern" section. Painfully unimposing structures bespeak progress in uniform drabness. Stark new monuments jut brashly from amid medieval ruins, vestiges of a gentler past. Faded yellow streetcars heavy with time shudder as they turn corners with a toneless screech. Pressburg, the once colorful, royal capital, is aging with an agonizing lack of grace. My initial excitement and apprehension are gradually melting into melancholy.

Bratislava, once known as Pressburg, had been the city of my happiest days. To me, the name itself was synonymous with the anticipation of adventure. Pressburg meant weekly shopping trips with my mother, excursions into a land of fun, a city of tall houses, wide avenues, brilliant toy stores, colorful candy shops. Where was the Katzburg candy factory sporting the Castle in miniature on its roof with a huge cat sprawled on top? Pressburg meant delicious restaurants where you could get the best hot dogs in the world. They were called *würstchen*, and were served with horseradish. In Pressburg bright red-and-yellow streetcars whizzed past you with such speed that all you saw were red or yellow streaks slashing the air. Horses' hooves clattered on the wide cobblestone streets as the ice or milk carts trotted by. And the intermittent sound of huge steamers greeting each other in the harbor made your heart grow faint with secret longing.

Mom always had words of praise for me in Pressburg. She used to say that I was very cooperative on the shopping trips she had to make for our store in Samorin. She said I was a good girl for holding her hand at busy intersections, for walking fast and not lingering at shop windows when she was in a hurry. She said I was a great help for carrying little parcels and never once losing them. Unlike my brother, I cooperated by not nagging for new toys and other trinkets. I was cooperative also by not pestering her with endless questions when she was busy talking to wholesalers and agents; I always waited patiently till the train ride home when she had time to listen to the questions and think about the answers. Oh, I had loved Pressburg!

Years later, after the war, Pressburg, now called Bratislava, was home. I lived in a girls' dormitory on Nesporova Street, and was familiar with every street, every landmark and statue in the numerous little pocket parks. In those years, while affection for the city had replaced my former awe, the city's magic did not dim. The cafés on the riverbank, the Gothic courtyards, the Castle on the hill, and the Coronation Church, remained sources of fascination. And pride. Bratislava remained the bastion of my expectations, the stronghold of my imagination.

In Bratislava, the people you passed on the street were more attractive than anywhere else, the students more intellectual, the artists more bohemian, the boys more handsome.

As a young teen, I found purpose for my life in Bratislava. I gained a passionate awareness of Jewish history, and shared with my fellow students the hope for a Jewish homeland, and a determination to struggle for its realization. Commitment to a cause was an integral part of the atmosphere in postwar Bratislava. The city, at the meeting point of East and West, and at the crossroads of three countries—Czechoslovakia, Hungary, and Austria—was vibrant and hospitable. It welcomed the young in need of a dream.

The bus approaches Avion Square, which is no longer on the outskirts of the city. Yet, all along the way, I have recognized nothing. Nothing, not a single sight, has struck a chord in my memory. What has become of my Bratislava—my life's central core? Where has it gone, this vital, cherished part of my life? Did it ever exist?

The bus comes to a halt. A dull, nagging sense of loss settles somewhere in my consciousness, and I begin to collect our things from the overhead rack.

"Where's your hat, Len? I can't see it anywhere."

Len hops on the seat to have a better look, finds his hat, and pops it on his head. I cannot suppress a smile. He looks every inch the casual tourist. As a matter of fact, "casual" is an understatement with Len. The hopelessly crushed hat lends him a look of eccentricity at best. Len's absolute lack of awareness of his appearance—his mistaken certainty that all is perfect—gives him a look of guileless innocence that

I have always found enchanting. Len catches my smile and his deep brown eyes light up for a moment. All at once, my crushing sense of loss is diminished.

"Where's your belt, Len?" He starts a hasty search for the belt of his raincoat. It is on the floor, and with an experienced tug Len retrieves it from under the foot of a rather overweight female passenger, startling her a bit.

One by one the passengers alight from the bus. As I reach the exit, I take a deep breath.

We have arrived.

CHAPTER TEN

The Bribe

On the platform, a woman with a shock of white hair and a wide-open smile is waving enthusiastically.

"Len, look—the lady with the white hair, waving—that must be Viola. She's come to meet us!"

"Really? That's a pleasant surprise," Len cries, adding reassuringly, "A good omen."

Viola was a native of Samorin but had left town when I was still a small child. Over a year ago, I had contacted her at the address Mom had received from her brother, and since then we had corresponded regularly about our project. Viola's warm offer of help had greatly encouraged me once I'd decided to undertake this mission.

"Hello, Viola. How nice of you to meet us."

A friendly robustness pervades Viola's greeting, and her warm, firm handshake provides us with a hearty welcome. I feel greatly encouraged. Next to Viola stands a tall, slender, dark-haired young woman.

"This is my daughter, Samira," Viola says, and Samira extends her hand to offer a shy, hesitant handshake. Just then Len emerges from behind the bus carrying a valise.

"This is my husband, Len. He does not speak Hungarian."

They all shake hands and Len mumbles something polite and unintelligible to compensate for not speaking the language. Samira smiles wanly and says nothing.

"Have you been waiting long? We were held up at the border. I'm sorry."

"No problem. We were happy to come," Viola says cheerfully.

Samira disappears without a word, and Viola explains apologetically: "Samira went to fetch the car. We could not park near the bus stop."

"I'm sorry for speaking Hungarian in Samira's company. My Slovak is a little rusty," I say. "I don't suppose Samira understood."

"Samira speaks Hungarian," Viola replies. "Hungarian is her mother tongue."

I am taken aback. "Hungarian—her mother tongue? What's happened to the ban against the Hungarian language?"

Viola seems offended by my remark. Her indignation is evident as she rises to the defense of her government: "There's total cultural freedom here. Minority cultures are respected and encouraged. I was a teacher in a Hungarian school, and Samira received a Hungarian education."

Just then Samira pulls up in a small red Skoda. She gets out and opens the *front* end, to reveal the trunk! Len puts the valises in the trunk and we are off.

"The Socialist system makes ample allowances for minority cultures," Viola says, picking up where she'd left off. "There are Hungarian newspapers, clubs, and organizations here. There is a Hungarian high school in Bratislava. There was even talk of a Hungarian university, but it did not materialize."

"Before I left here, thirty-odd years ago, no one was allowed to speak Hungarian openly. When did that change happen?" I ask.

"Socialism does not tolerate primitive nationalistic animosities. Hungary is a fellow Socialist state. We have mutual trade agreements, cultural cooperation, all kinds of common ventures. I, for instance, declared my nationality as Hungarian. Therefore I can demand Hungarian cultural privileges. It was my privilege to give my daughter a Hungarian education."

How could everything have changed so drastically? Somewhere, there must be a cloud to this silver lining. What about the "primitive nationalistic animosity" vis-à-vis Israel?

I feel bad for Len, with all of this conversation in a foreign language. I translate a summary of the conversation, but know that we have a language problem on our hands. Samira drives without having uttered a word.

The car stops in front of a nondescript building, one of the many "modern" structures we passed on our way into the city.

"We are home," Viola declares, and produces a large key for the front entrance. She ushers us through a dark and somewhat dank hallway to the elevator. The four of us cram into the rickety conveyance with our valises. With a sudden lurch and an audible groan, the elevator stops on the third floor and we gratefully file out of its confinement.

"We are home!" Viola declares for the second time as she swings open the door to their apartment.

The salon is airy and large but overstuffed with heavy dark furniture and masses of draperies, cushions, and knickknacks. At a little ornate table, the two hostesses serve tea and biscuits. Viola is still effusive and Samira, still silent and withdrawn. When Samira finally speaks, her Hungarian is impeccable but accented with Slovak. Her voice is soft and cultured, and as she grows more relaxed, a touch of humor sparkles through. As she continues to warm up, Samira admits that she speaks English. Her English is grammatical and her vocabulary is very good, and I breathe a sigh of relief. Samira is entertaining Len, and I am free to discuss our plans with Viola.

"There are several difficulties so far. Things I could not write to you about," Viola begins. "For one thing, the commissar in Samorin refuses to issue a permit for the exhumation without a power-of-attorney signed by all the surviving relatives. He insists on that. He claims he wants no trouble from other relatives who would perhaps show up at some future date and claim the bodies."

"What a bizarre assumption!" I exclaim.

But Viola sympathizes with the commissar. "Well, one can understand his concern," she says somewhat defensively. "He wants to be covered; he's entitled to that. Without the commissar's permit we cannot proceed."

"But I have a permit from Prague, from the Ministry of Foreign Affairs."

"I understand. But this is not Prague. Here you'll need the local commissar's permit. And with that you'll have to apply to the state burial commission for a permit to carry out the exhumation—the opening of the graves and all the other tasks associated with it. It is this office that issues orders to gravediggers, coffin makers, hearse drivers, and other workers involved in the process. Here individuals cannot hire these workers. Only the state can assign these jobs."

"Now, let me get this straight," I say. "The Samorin commissar's permit is a prerequisite for the permit of the burial commission. And the commissar won't issue a permit without a power-of-attorney signed by all surviving descendants of my grandparents . . . but I have no such document in my possession," I say in a low voice, to mask my rising alarm. "So the commissar's permit is out, and the burial commission's permit is out . . ."

In order to contain my distress, I assume a matter-of-fact tone of practicality. "Our first task, then, is to obtain the power-of-attorney the commissar in Samorin is demanding."

"Not the first, actually,"Viola says with some hesitation. "There is yet another. A permit from the Ministry of Health is a prerequisite, as you'd call it, for the permit from the commissar in Samorin. You see, exhumation of bodies up to twenty-five years after burial is considered a health hazard . . ."

"Ah, but my grandparents died over fifty years ago."

"I know—and you're right. There shouldn't be a problem,"Viola remarks in a conciliatory tone. "I myself was quite surprised when I discovered this last year, when my brother and I made arrangements for the exhumation of my father's body."

It was Viola's brother who had told Mother about the impending flood of the Samorin Jewish cemetery. Now Viola relates the tale of their own predicament with the opening of their father's grave. Her tale contains a welcome surprise for me. I had not known that the grave of Viola's father was adjacent to my grandfather's, and in the course of preparing for the exhumation of her father's bones—which included clearing a path to the tomb, as well as the area, cutting down trees and underbrush—Viola and her brother had found my grandparents' graves underneath the forest-like growth that covered even the tallest monument in the graveyard.

"You mentioned nothing about this in your correspondence," I marvel. "How strange. I've been making arrangements for the exhumation for two years now, and had no idea I might not ever find the graves. I had no idea the entire cemetery has turned into a wild forest, obscuring the tombstones."

"The cemetery's near the Danube,"Viola explains. "The river fertilizes the soil for miles, and the vegetation is very lush near there. The grass and underbrush grew unchecked for decades . . ."

The Danube—this river that had shaped my life—was shaping my life still. It brought me back to the place I'd been trying to erase from my memory for years. Because of the Danube the tombs of my ancestors had been engulfed by the forest, threatened by oblivion under its waters, and now they have emerged as if by magic from the sea of vegetation . . . just in time for my mission.

"When the commissariat in Samorin insisted on a health permit in my father's case," Viola goes on, "I traveled to Dunajska Streda and applied for the permit at the Ministry of Health, even though I knew the law, and knew that my father had been buried more than twenty-five years. The Ministry of Health denied my application precisely on these grounds. The denial stated that because my father had been buried for over twenty-five years, the health permit was redundant. And they refused to issue a redundant document." Viola's discomfort at revealing this is evident. Yet she continues: "In desperation I went to the library, looked up the law, made copies, and took them to the commissar in Samorin as written proof of the redundancy of his demand. He read it, then shook his head, smiled, and said that he could not help me. Without the permit from the Ministry of Health, he was not authorized to issue a permit for the exhumation."

"But this is insane," I exclaim.

Viola goes on in a monotonous fashion: "I pleaded with top officials at the Ministry of Health who knew me from the early days of the Party. To no avail. They said that it was against their Socialist principles to issue a redundant piece of paper. I could not argue with that."

"What did you do, for God's sake?"

"I went to see an old comrade in the Party, a friend of the Health Ministry bigwig. He's a high-ranking member of the Central Bureau, and he addressed a letter of introduction to the commissar in Samorin. The letter referred to my past as a freedom fighter and to my position in the Founders' Commissariat. I thought our troubles were over. I was wrong. The commissar said he was honored to make my acquaintance but could not disobey the rules."

"What rules?"

"One doesn't ask questions like that. For me this was especially awkward because of my brother Alfred. Alfred came from Australia for the express purpose of the exhumation. Alfred is a capitalist and a religious fanatic. He's always mocked the Socialist system. Do you know what he said? He said that there was a simple solution to this dilemma: money. He said it was obvious the commissar wanted a bribe. I was enraged. I told him his corrupt capitalist methods had no place here.

"The next morning he announced that he wanted to take matters into his own hands. Later in the day, he returned with the news that he'd found a contact man who would slip a few hundred dollars into the proper hands, making the whole machinery run smoothly. 'Oil money,' he called it. A high-ranking official at the Health Ministry was the contact. He would start the 'grease job' at his end.

"I was horrified, but there was nothing I could do. I had reached a dead end. You cannot imagine my shock when two days later Alfred arrived from Samorin with the permit from the commissar in his hands. You cannot begin to understand how I felt. Anyway, now I know the method. I know the contact man, and I've already made an appointment for you. Tomorrow morning at seven, at his home in Dunajska Streda."

"Tomorrow morning! But it's past midnight. How can we make it there by seven in the morning?"

"There is a 5:00 a.m. bus that takes workers to Samorin, and from Samorin there are frequent buses to Dunajska Streda. You should make it by seven. Let me give you the address of the contact."

While Viola is rummaging for the address in her chest of drawers, I have a sudden thought: "Viola, would Samira consent to drive us to Dunajska Streda?" I ask. Samira had retired to her room, and Len had fallen asleep on the sofa. "We would compensate her for all expenses, including a day's wages."

Viola seems pleased with the proposal. "But I must speak to Samira first," she warns. "It depends on her." After a brief consultation, Viola emerges from the side room, happy to report that the idea also appeals to Samira. I am pleased with the news, and so is Len when I wake him gently and advise him of the latest plan.

Viola offers to come along, and the mission takes on an element of excitement.

At 5:00 a.m., coffee is perking in the kitchen. On a crisp white tablecloth, rolls, butter, green peppers, and gooseberries are laid out. In the bathroom I strap the money belt Mother had made for the journey, with pockets for foreign currency, about my waist. In each pocket I slip wads of U.S. dollars, German marks, Austrian shillings, and some British pounds. Checks and credit cards are meaningless in the anticapitalist paradise behind the Iron Curtain. With the various currencies peeping out of the pockets, the money belt presents a colorful sight. I have no way of knowing which color of cash is most likely to buy Communist favors.

CHAPTER ELEVEN

The Drive

IN THE HEAVY COMMERCIAL TRAFFIC THE RED SKODA KEEPS TO A NARROW line.

"Soon the open fields will come into view," I explain to Len, and the anticipation flushes warmth through my body. "As soon as we leave the outskirts of the city, you'll see fields of wheat and corn, a wavy yellow expanse stretching to the horizon . . ."

The car moves on the open road. No cornfields for several miles. Instead, a lunar landscape with hundreds of enormous gray, circular shapes with tall cylindrical projections unfolding on both sides of the road.

"Viola, what are those structures?"

"This is an oil refinery—the largest in the Eastern Bloc," Viola answers.

"Oil refinery? Here? Since when are there oil wells in Czechoslovakia?"

"There are no oil wells here. This is a refinery for Soviet oil. Belongs to the Soviet Union," Viola explains. "Crude oil is pumped here through pipelines across the continent, refined here, and pumped back into the Soviet Union."

"But why such enormous distances? Why pump oil so far west and not refine it nearer to home?"

"Czechoslovakia provides the space and the expertise," Viola replies, then falls silent. After a brief pause she goes on, without answering my question. "There was a lot of opposition here to the project.

It's polluting our air. Can you imagine the extent of pollution caused by such a mammoth plant smack in the middle of a densely populated area, wedged in between villages? And it destroyed our farmlands. Now there's not a patch of agricultural space between Bratislava and Samorin. Not a single patch of green. Neither vegetable groves nor grain fields. Perhaps you remember that this region, the Small Lower Plain, had been the most fertile in the country. Do you remember your geography? This was called the fruit bowl and the grain basin of the entire country." Viola, the teacher, is in her element.

"Of course I remember." I translate for Len.

The car speeds on the open highway and the lunar landscape seems to stretch to infinity.

"You see, not an inch of meadowland. No grazing fields and no herds." Viola's voice once again takes on a monotonous quality. "We fought it by every means at our disposal. We knew that the blight of this fruitful plain would mean the devastation of our economy. The people around here had been farmers for centuries. Their entire way of life was farming, their customs, rituals, their courtship, even the manner of burying their dead. Their philosophy of life was shaped by their crops growing out of the soil. Take away their farms and they are dead."

"Then what happened?"

"You see what happened. The Soviet Union won. The oil refinery was built right under our kitchen windows. Thousand of homes were demolished, together with gardens and meadows, to make room for this monstrous plant. Some farmers are employed by the refinery. Others commute great distances to industrial centers, mostly as unskilled labor. Many others left their families in search of employment as far away as Moravia and Bohemia. The entire social structure of the region was destroyed."

As I translate for Len, he is aghast. "It makes no sense," he says. "It seems an awful waste, and counterproductive."

"The damage is inestimable," Viola continues. "As time goes on, the blight spreads beyond the immediate region. Fruit and grain production has been drastically reduced even in the areas not immediately involved, because of the fumes the plant expels into the atmosphere."

Samira fidgets uneasily in the driver's seat, and Viola falls silent. Has she revealed too much? Too much information, or too much feeling of resentment? I want the two women to know that I appreciate their position and would never abuse their confidence. By way of reassurance I say: "Perhaps it's not as bad as you think. Perhaps in the long run it's for the best."

Viola understands the implication. She says: "Samira doesn't like it when I talk this way. Not because you're from the West. She doesn't like me to talk this way even when we are alone."

"Because there's no point," Samira says quietly. This is the first time she has spoken since we left Bratislava. "There's no point. There's nothing we can do about these things. Why talk about them? What's the point?" She drives on silently, her eyes on the road.

But Viola's inner turmoil bursts forth again in a torrent of angry words.

"The fruit and vegetable export to the Soviet Union did not diminish. We're expected to deliver our quota—and we do. We continue to supply a substantial share of the food for the Soviets, just like before. The blight of our farmlands is no excuse as far as the Soviets are concerned. Tons of fruit and vegetables are shipped out of here daily. And we have serious shortages, especially now, during the Olympics. We have to ship them more food now, so that the Soviet Union is able to present a front of plenty to the world, the West especially. It's extremely important for them that the West should see how plentiful their food supply is despite their great technological advances. Our tomatoes and melons are resplendent on the fruit stands of Moscow, but have you seen a piece of fruit here? Well, you've just arrived. The green peppers we had for breakfast I grew in my own little garden. Years ago, I applied for a small patch I spotted between two buildings on Spitalska Street, and last year I received the permit to cultivate it. I grow green peppers, tomatoes, and gooseberries. I take the bus there almost every day to work in that garden."

"Len and I loved your gooseberries at breakfast. They were very sweet."

"Gooseberries are no novelty here. For some strange reason, they are the only fruit that's not shipped to the Soviet Union. But you'll not see a single peach, apple, pear, apricot, or plum here—or tomatoes, cucumbers, or green peppers. Do you remember the kind of pears, peaches, and apricots we used to have? They were the specialty of our region. Ah, my mother used to make tons of jam. August was jam month."

"I remember well. My mother started in July and went on 'jamming' till the holidays."

How well I remember huge cauldrons bubbling over with sweet, sticky jam. I hated those months. The house was packed with crates of fruit, the kitchen cluttered with jam jars, containers of sugar, and the white powder for preservative . . . what was its name? Salicyl. Oh, yes, salicyl, the white chemical with a cloying smell.

"I've not seen a peach, an apple, an apricot . . . for years," Viola complains. She turns around in her seat, looks me square in the face, and poses a question as if it were a philosophical theorem: "Can you describe an apricot?"

"I'll send you a snapshot from Israel," I quip, and immediately regret my remark. But Viola does not mind. She gives a chuckle. Her robust good nature wins out, and the cycle of bitterness is broken. She goes on in a lighter mood.

"We've been told, months in advance, that we must cooperate in this vital project of prime ideological importance. During the Olympics we must show the West that our consumer goods and agricultural produce are on par with theirs. So our cucumbers, tomatoes, and peaches are doing the job there, I hope. The foreigners are sampling our fruit, and I hope they are duly impressed. And the residents of Samorin, Usor, Mliecno, Bratislava, Komarno, and all the rest of the region can sample only their memories of the fruit."

"There are gooseberries here. Gooseberries are a lovely fruit," I interject, still fearful that Viola will regret her words too late to retract them. "I haven't eaten gooseberries since I left Czechoslovakia. Neither has Leonard, since his childhood in Ireland. There are no gooseberries where we live in America, nor in Israel."

"You'll have your fill here," Viola says sarcastically.

The oil refinery is behind us. But even here there is not an inch of open space; the outskirts of one village reach the outskirts of the next. It seems as if this area is nothing but the industrial backwoods of Bratislava, an extension of the Slovak capital.

Viola confirms my impression. "As a matter of fact, there's a project to incorporate all the villages till Samorin, and Samorin itself, into the municipality of Bratislava."

"Speak of the devil!" Viola exclaims as we whiz past a small sign with the name SAMORIN. My heart skips a beat. The car passes a bus station on the right, and a few small two-story buildings on both sides of the highway, followed by a stretch of open road.

"So we're near Samorin. Does the highway bisect the town?"

"We've passed Samorin," Samira says without removing her gaze from the road. "Haven't you seen the sign?"

"I've seen the sign, but . . ."

"That was Samorin," Samira says with a chuckle. "Actually, the Bratislava-Dunajska Streda highway passes the outskirts of the town. We're headed straight for Dunajska Streda." She glances at her watch. "We're behind schedule. It's six forty-five and we're still far from D.S. The trip has taken longer than I'd estimated. I admit such a long drive is a new experience for me. I'm a new driver."

"You're doing fine. Don't worry—I'm sure the contact person won't mind waiting a few minutes to put his sticky fingers on corrupt Western cash," I say.

The two women in the front seat do not appreciate my humor. They are silent, but Len laughs out loud after I translate.

Signposts whiz by, names of villages. This is the road on which thirty-five years ago, we—Mother, Aunt Serena, Bubi, and I—were driven like doomed cattle to the collection point in the Dunajska Streda synagogue compound. Father was no longer with us. This road was the beginning of the end. Each village was a landmark to our doom.

The sign DUNAJSKA STREDA pops into view, and Samira calls out happily: "Good. We are here. Not too bad; after all it's only five past seven. We are not too late."

Tall, stark buildings line the empty streets with huge red stars on rooftops. Sparse, commercial traffic dappled here and there by a horse-drawn cart. But no people anywhere. Not a single soul on the streets.

Where are the people? The people from the sidewalks, the doorways, the windows? The people with large, cold eyes, staring . . . Have they vanished?

CHAPTER TWELVE

The Beginning of the End

APRIL 1944

THE PEOPLE CROWD THE STREETS; SIDEWALKS AND DOORWAYS ARE CRAMMED with men, women, and children. They all stare . . . They gaze through the windows, from behind storefronts, from balconies . . .

I see them from the corners of my eyes. I see their gaze grow larger and larger, growing with every street we pass. Now the crowd is one gigantic stare. A gigantic, voracious stare seems to swallow our cart.

The cart floats as if in a dream. Soon we'll arrive at the synagogue. Soon this agonizing stare will be behind us. Soon we'll be safely behind the tall fence of the synagogue compound.

"Don't look sideways," Mommy whispers between clenched teeth. "Keep your eyes straight ahead."

She sits next to me, erect and pale, a stone statue. Mommy is invisible behind the white skin, the perfectly chiseled profile, and the absolutely still posture. She emanates the tragic quiet of a marble monument. How beautiful she is . . .

I cannot see Bubi and Aunt Serena. Their cart is too far ahead. How much longer will this agonizing drive along the streets last? When will the endless stare be over? When will we get to the synagogue?

From the corner of my eye, I can see shuttered shops. There's Mr. Grunwald's dry goods store. There's Weiss & Co. Textiles. And the delicatessen, Brandwein & Sons. The store is shuttered but I can smell the delicious fragrance of smoked beef. Why are all these stores shuttered?

Fear like a thin, slimy snake crawls into my belly.

"Sit still," Mommy whispers.

Sit still. Turn into a stone statue. Stone statues do not feel. Stone statues do not see the stares. They face ahead, not seeing, not hearing, not speaking. Only waiting. When will this be over? When will we be off the street?

The row of laden, horse-drawn carts comes to a stop. But where's the synagogue? We are not at the synagogue yet.

"Why did we stop here?" I ask Mommy, my voice shattering the silence like a thin sheet of glass.

The coachman replies in an unexpectedly gruff voice: "We wait here for the others to unload."

One by one, the carts unload their cargo of men, women, children, bundles, and baby carriages. One by one, we inch ahead. Bit by bit the sprawling, familiar synagogue building comes into view. Inch by inch our cart is aligned with the entrance of the synagogue yard.

Mother descends with stiff, deliberate movements and gives me a hand. I am dizzy. I clamber down the cart with some difficulty and join the crowd on the sidewalk.

The sidewalk teems with a multitude in motion. We spot Aunt Serena and Bubi, and join them. The four of us become part of the inexorable human flood sweeping through the open gates of the synagogue yard.

Daddy, where are you now? How I wish I could feel your hand on my shoulder. Daddy, I am afraid. I step over bodies in the synagogue yard. I must step carefully, as a human carpet covers the entire yard. The sun is blinding; there are little children under my feet. I am stepping on hands, on feet.

Who are these people under my feet? "Where have all these people come from?" I ask aloud, half shrieking.

"We are from here, from the town," a voice answers. "We were brought in here this morning. All the Jews of this town, and many others from the surrounding countryside."

"But that's impossible!" I shriek. "There are thousands of Jews in this town!"

"Move on," Mommy urges from behind. "Move on, faster. You must not stop. There are many people behind us."

The human carpet is in constant motion. I am terribly dizzy, but I forge ahead, right behind my brother. I am focusing on the knapsack on his back so as not to lose him. I must also focus on where I'm stepping so as not to trip and fall on top of anybody.

"Don't be scared," Mom says without emotion. "Just move a little faster."

We reach the synagogue steps. The steps, too, are covered with live bodies. The entrance hall is crammed. Bubi heads for the staircase and I follow, picking my way among sprawling bodies, up and up, to the ladies' gallery, which is crammed with people.

"The attic," Bubi says, and I balance my heavy bundle even higher on the crowded stairs.

It's dark and stifling hot in the attic. Within seconds, prone bodies emerge from the darkness.

"There's an empty spot here," Mother says, and spreads the blanket. "Enough for at least two." Aunt Serena drops her bundle and sits on it. Bubi continues to grope in the dark and finds an empty nook for himself hidden under the low gabled roof.

Through a gap among the tiles, I can see a world of rooftops, a strange, forbidding world. Suddenly the world below seems unfamiliar, as if we no longer belonged to it. It seems so far away and removed. From up here in the attic of the synagogue the world seems frightfully distant and unapproachable.

Aunt Serena now lies lifeless on the blanket, her head propped by a rolled-up towel, her eyes closed. On her forehead there are dewdrops of sweat, and on her left temple a little blood vessel keeps throbbing, the only signs of life. I pull a towel from the bundle and begin to fan her with it. She opens her eyes: "Don't exhaust yourself, sweetheart," she whispers. "You, too, must be very tired."

"I'm not tired," I lie, as I continue fanning my beloved aunt.

Mom is fumbling in her bundle for the food parcel.

"I'm not hungry," Bubi says.

"I'm terribly thirsty," I whisper, and Mommy retrieves an empty jug from the bundle. "I'll scout for water," she says without emotion.

Aunt Serena closes her eyes again. Her thin body is motionless. Her bony chest heaves with every breath. As I kneel beside my darling aunt and move my hand in rhythm with her breathing, I spot another gap in the tiles. I can see the world of rooftops for miles.

The new, indifferent, forbidding world, and its hostile stare . . .

CHAPTER THIRTEEN

Buying Favors

WE DRIVE THROUGH DESERTED STREETS UNTIL WE REACH A CORNER WHERE A group of workers is congregating. Samira calls out to them: "Can you direct us to the hospital?" The workers look at each other helplessly. Not one responds. Then one of them hesitantly approaches the car and asks in broken Slovak: "Can you speak Hungarian?"

When Samira repeats her question in Hungarian, a sudden charge is infused into the group. They all gesticulate and talk at once and point out the way. Samira thanks them and we take off.

"How is it possible that they don't speak Slovak? Aren't these men from around here?"

"Of course they are," Viola answers. "But Dunajska Streda retained its Hungarian character, just like other towns in the area. The local people speak Hungarian. There are Hungarian schools. Priests preach in Hungarian, and the civil servants are bilingual. The Hungarians have no compulsion to learn the language of the state."

There is no point in telling Viola about the ruthless crackdown on the Hungarian language during the immediate postwar period. She was not here then and would not believe it. The Slovaks understood that language was the key to territory. This region has been forever disputed because of the language spoken by the inhabitants. It had been claimed and finally annexed by Hungary during the war because of its "Hungarian" character. After the war the Slovak authorities were determined to solve the ethnic problem once and for all: In one sweep they deported the Magyar gentry and all "pure" Hungarians to Hungary and imported ethnic Slovaks to take their place. The others who remained, mostly landless peasants and artisans, were warned: shape up or ship out. This is Slovakia now; either learn the language and teach it to your children, or leave. Many did the latter. Voluntarily, they followed their fellow Magyars to an unknown fate in Hungary rather than learn the Slovak language and adopt Slovak ways. They feared for their culture rather than their stomachs, and during the early postwar years they crossed the Danube to the Hungarian side in droves.

This was almost four decades ago. When did the change take place—and why?

The Skoda comes to a stop in front of a well-tended garden.

"This is it," Samira said with a mixture of pride and relief. It is 7:10 a.m. The sign on the door says IGOR RADEK in bold, black letters. Viola rings the bell.

A congenial-looking gentleman with a shock of a white mustache opens the door and invites us to enter. The anteroom is lined with shelves full of knickknacks. Comrade Radek opens a heavy oak door to the parlor and we file through in awkward silence.

Viola makes the introductions and Comrade Radek bids us to sit around an oblong oak table polished to a deep brown glow. We sit on heavy oak chairs in a room lined with dark brown shelves stacked with books bound in brown leather, and more knickknacks. Everything is brown, except for Mr. Radek's mustache, which moves in mild contrast against the soft brown immobility of the room as he keeps nodding during Viola's detailed recitation of our case. Finally Viola comes to the point:

"My friend and her spouse came here in order to express their gratitude for your help in this matter. They realize the Commissariat's understandable reluctance to permit removal of citizens' remains from their native soil, and they truly regret taking such a course of action. It is done, however, in compliance with the explicit wishes of my friend's mother, who is the daughter of the deceased citizens in question. She is an expatriate, and for many years a citizen of the United States of America, in which land she now wishes to have her parents reburied."

Poor Mother; she is made out to be the heavy in this farce. How much longer will this charade go on?

Comrade Radek nods again, and says that he understands our predicament. But, he adds with delicate tact, he feels obliged to point out the complexities of the case and to warn us of unforeseen difficulties. He advises us to exercise extreme caution. Then, after an awkward pause, he hints with obvious discomfort that the cost of permits for such procedures has risen and he is "compelled to request" a somewhat larger sum than previously.

Before Viola can formulate a convoluted reply, I interject: "How much?"

As if simultaneously stung by twin snakes, Comrade Radek and Viola gasp in unison. I have committed the unforgivable: Directness in negotiations of any kind was an unpardonable offense here. To make it worse, the mention of money constituted a capital breech. The room is suspended in dead silence. Finally Comrade Radek exhales a painful, barely audible whisper: "Three hundred."

"Three hundred what?" I ask. "What currency?"

"Dollars," the comrade mutters, and the dewdrops that had precipitated on his brow now begin a sudden lurch toward his spectacular mustache. But I am relentless in my insistence on plain talk: "May I ask what this money is for? Is this the fee for the health permit? Or is it to cover all costs?"

Viola clears her throat. The comrade fixes his gaze on the tabletop and gives no indication of having heard my question. Viola and Samira sit as if paralyzed. Len's face is an open question.

What have I done? Have I gone too far? Have I ruined everything?

"Excuse me," I interject into the vacuum, and hurriedly leave the brown morass of despondency. In the anteroom, I dislodge three notes damp with sweat from the money belt under my skirt and reenter the room. Without speaking, I place the folded notes on the polished brown tabletop in front of the comrade. A crimson blush spreads to the comrade's scalp. With a slow, deliberate motion he lifts the bills from the table and slips them into his pocket. Then he rises.

"We must reach Comrade Doctor Hurok before he leaves his office," he says tonelessly. "It's eight-thirty. He leaves around nine."

Comrade Radek and I walk briskly along a narrow dirt road leading to the hospital while the others wait in the car. A large red star above the entrance proclaims that the neat, unassuming structure is a state institution. Comrade Radek ushers me along a whitewashed corridor until we reach a curtained glass door. Here Comrade Radek knocks, then enters, leaving me with a muttered apology in the corridor. A few minutes later, he comes out and bids me into Dr. Hurok's office. A tall man with a gray Vandyke and blue eyes rises from his desk, and Comrade Radek introduces me to him in Hungarian.

"This is the American lady who hails from our parts," he says, and Dr. Hurok clicks his heels, makes a ceremonious bow, and extends his hand. "I am Dr. Hurok," he says with a flourish. "I am at your service, madam."

Such chivalry? Which forgotten nook of the Communist system had preserved this vestige of prewar Hungarian courtesies? Dr. Hurok holds my chair until I am seated. Now Comrade Radek reviews my tale in formal detail, similar to Viola's earlier recitation. While the comrade speaks, Dr. Hurok keeps nodding approval: "Ah, yes. Yes. Go on, please, Comrade. Go on. Of course. Of course."

When Comrade Radek finishes speaking, Dr. Hurok flashes a ceremonious but amiable smile in my direction. "I am delighted to be of service in this matter. I am almost sure this can be arranged."

Now the two men launch into an excited discussion in rapid Slovak, which seems to go on forever. When it finally ends, Dr. Hurok leaves the room. Radek and I are left alone for about twenty minutes, during which the comrade reassures me that Dr. Hurok was a very important man and would attend to the matter personally. He stresses the word "personally."

Dr. Hurok returns and asks for my documents, including my American passport. He peruses the passport very closely, and a frown begins forming on his forehead. My apprehension grows. He examines all the documents one by one, and once more scrutinizes the passport. My apprehension turns into panic that rises to my throat.

Dr. Hurok then abruptly springs to his feet, puts a piece of paper in the typewriter on a nearby desk, sinks into a chair, and begins to type. He types on for almost an hour, laboriously using two fingers, alternately frowning and holding brief consultations with the comrade. Now it is after ten. What has happened to his nine o'clock appointment?

Suddenly Dr. Hurok springs to his feet again, and declares: "This is it!"

Comrade Radek eagerly scales the distance between them in one leap and glances at the typed page: "Yes. You've got it. It's perfect."

"Now we may proceed," Dr. Hurok announces. "The rest is easy. Now I might as well type the final draft. In triplicate. What do you think?" he turns to the comrade.

"Of course, Comrade Doctor. You know best."

Dr. Hurok puts a thick sandwich of typing paper and carbon sheets in the antiquated typewriter and sets to work. Half an hour later the permit is ready, and the two men hail it, once again. Then Dr. Hurok makes an unexpected declaration: He would personally escort "our American guest," first to the Customs Authority here, to make sure the document falls into the "proper hands," and after that, he would accompany "the gracious American lady" all the way to Samorin and present her to the "proper" authorities.

Comrade Radek is visibly pleased with this turn of events, and I express my gratitude. Samira's little Skoda is to be our transport. Viola has to stay behind to make room for Dr. Hurok in the front seat. Suddenly congenial Comrade Radek offers to entertain Viola during our absence.

CHAPTER FOURTEEN

Louis the Madman of Samorin

"I MISSED YOU," LEN WHISPERS AS SOON AS WE FIND OURSELVES IN THE RELA-
tive privacy of the car's backseat. I realize how lonely all this must be
for Len. The language barrier, and my involvement with these people
in lengthy, incomprehensible maneuverings, has erected an invisible
wall of isolation around him.

I find the small paper bag of gooseberries Viola had prepared for
the journey, and pop one in Len's mouth. We laugh, and I begin to
update him on all that has been happening. I talk rapidly to make it
difficult for Dr. Hurok to listen in. He knows some English. He told
me how his father, a former university professor, had insisted on introducing foreign languages into the home. Dr. Hurok's upper-middle-
class birth must have hindered his advancement in the Communist
system. Viola had told me of the extent to which birth determined
one's place in the Communist order. Viola's own middle-class background was not held against her; her long years of ideological dedi-
cation more than counterbalanced it. Despite her roots, Viola was
recognized as a true Socialist. Dr. Hurok did not possess those credentials. The son of the "capitalist" system's intellectual elite had to
consider himself fortunate with his small-town civil service position,
while men with inferior qualifications, but with the appropriate pro-
letarian background, occupied positions of eminence.

As it turns out, I have no cause for concern about Dr. Hurok
eavesdropping on our chat. He and Samira hit it off well, and soon

they are deep in lively conversation, giving Len and myself a chance to restore our sorely missed intimacy.

"I want to know about everything that's going on," Len says, putting his arm about my shoulders while his eyes scan the flat countryside. "I want to know your impressions about everything, all of the places we're passing. Do you remember any of them?"

In the distance church steeples, grain silos, and red-roofed houses float in and out of view, followed by stretches of wide-open, green-patched meadow. Billboards with vaguely familiar names of villages whiz by us on the roadside. Road signs with half-remembered messages dance among the telephone poles. It is like a scene from a long-forgotten dream.

"There's a faint familiarity about it all. I know I've been here; I know I've seen all of this before. But I don't remember anything in particular—as if it all happened in another lifetime."

As I say this, a twinge of loss digs deep in my consciousness. I watch a long masonry fence follow a scattering of farmhouses and a familiar white steeple tower above a cluster of taller buildings.

"That church steeple I remember—that's the Lutheran church. This must be Samorin."

"Didn't you see the sign for Samorin?" Len asks. "We passed it some time ago."

Dr. Hurok is directing Samira to an open square in the center of the town. The building facing the square . . . it's the town hall, still painted a drab olive green. And there, across the square at a right angle to the town hall . . . It's the high school building, still yellow. The flagpole is still tilted at a crazy angle. A low cast-iron fence encloses the small park in the middle of the square, just like before. But that gray building next to the school with white window frames and an enormous red star—that was not there before. Neither was the monument in the center, a fierce-looking military figure in dark metal.

Dr. Hurok holds open the car door. "Here, madam. We must hurry, I'm afraid. The offices at city hall close at noon. We barely have time," he says, and advises Samira about possible parking spaces behind the marketplace.

Len remains in the car, and I follow Dr. Hurok as he dashes up the front stairs and through the wide entrance of the building. Once inside, we race up a flight of stairs and along a narrow corridor. Dr. Hurok reaches a double door on the right, and after an urgent knock, flings it wide open. In the office he greets the clerks with a breezy wave of his hand and asks to be announced to the city commissar.

One of the clerks returns with the announcement that the commissar is expecting us. My stomach gives a sudden lurch: Who knows if the "oil money" managed to trickle to this city commissar's office yet?

From the front office teeming with clerks, we proceed through several interceding rooms, and with every anteroom we cross, with every room that precedes his office, the commissar appears to me more and more formidable.

Dr. Hurok holds the heavy door, and I walk self-consciously into the commissar's office. Behind the massive desk sits—a woman! She seems massive as well, and as she stands to shake hands with the two of us, the large body, solid neck, and strong face look as if they are hewn out of rock. A calm dignity pervades the space about her. There is no forbidding harshness in that space. Her mien conveys a comfortable aura of authority. I like this woman. I sense that the commissar will not make this difficult for me.

I am right. When Dr. Hurok presents my case and hands her the papers, the commissar nods, then signs and stamps the document without comment.

"Just a moment," she says, then rises and leaves the room.

"Here comes the tough part," Dr. Hurok whispers. "One more official has to countersign it. This commissar is okay, but I don't know about the other. Some like to be difficult."

The commissar returns with the document. "Here," she says, turning to me. "This is your permit for the exhumation."

"That's it?" I ask, unbelieving.

"Yes. Take this to the *Pohrebny Ustav*. The rest is up to them."

"That's the Burial Authority," Dr. Hurok explains in Hungarian.

"Your language is Hungarian?" the commissar asks, with a simplicity that conveys the same comfortable sense of authority, even warmth.

"Yes. I was born and grew up in this town," I answer, and suddenly find myself choking with emotion. "And you? Are you from here?"

"I was not born here," she says. "But I have lived here for over twenty-five years. My husband was born here."

"Who is your husband? What's his name?" I ask, and the choking sensation intensifies. "You see, I would like to know if any of my friends, the people I grew up with . . . if any of them is around."

Suddenly, inexplicably, I am fighting tears. I am mortified.

The commissar's voice is soft as she answers: "My husband's family name is Lengyel. He is Peter Lengyel."

"Peti Lengyel? From Landowners' Row?"

"Yes. Peti's family used to live on Landowners' Row. It no longer exists; it was demolished years ago. There's a city block in its place. And Peti's family is gone, to 'the other side.' "

Peti, the gawky kid with long ears like a rabbit. He always helped me carry the milk can, swinging it a little, and when the foaming white liquid surged over the rim, he giggled. Papa shouted from the store entrance, "Look out, Peti, you're spilling the milk," and slipped a coin into Peti's palm. Peti ran like a rabbit up the hill to the white farmhouse on Landowners' Row, and Papa smiled and my heart almost burst with happiness . . .

I clear my throat. "Your husband's family, Comrade Commissar, and my family, we were neighbors. You wouldn't know the Friedmann house. That was our house, on the corner, across the hill from the Lengyel farm."

"I know the Friedmann house; it's still standing," the commissar says with a hint of animation in her voice. "The large yellow house on the corner of Main Street, facing Freedom Square. The store sign was removed years ago, but people still call it Friedmann Corner. The farmsteads and the farmers are gone. There are three-story town houses in their place, with new people in them. From the other side."

Her voice lowers as she says this. Is it caution that makes the commissar lower her voice, or is it sadness and resentment? Perhaps all three. Whatever the reason, as she is engaged in conversation with me, this strong, dignified woman is no longer the city commissar of Samorin.

"There are very few old-timers left in Samorin," she adds. "When we were first married, I met most of Peti's family and friends. Then most were resettled on the other side."

"What about Peti's uncle, Louis? What became of him?"

Mad Louis never spoke to anyone, never noticed anyone. He used to sit in front of the white farmhouse on top of the hill, his back straight as an arrow, and in a sonorous, high-pitched singsong, he'd recite the Bible from dawn to dusk. We children were petrified of Mad Louis and his weird chant and dared not approach the hill when he sat there, upright like an apparition. Once, on a dare, I tiptoed behind his back and discovered that he was not reading from the Bible at all but from a crumpled piece of paper he held in his hand. And his chant was but a string of nonsensical syllables. No one believed me when I revealed this, yet no one ever dared to check it out.

"Oh, he died before we were married. I never met him."

"I can't imagine the hill without him."

"There is no hill. It was leveled, along with Landowners' Row."

Comrade Commissar smiles sadly as she says this, and suddenly I realize she is sad for me. Not for the hill and Landowners' Row and the Lengyels, who together with all the Hungarian landowners were deported to Hungary, to the "other side" of the Danube. That happened a long, long time ago. She is sad for *me*, the American woman who returned to confront her childhood and has just found out that her childhood had vanished almost without a trace. Little did the commissar know that the postwar political upheaval swallowed all but a few spare vestiges of that childhood. That childhood had vanished violently long ago . . . and yet it was still intact, still alive and insistent, intruding upon every dream, upon every waking moment.

"My greetings to your husband, Comrade Commissar. And I thank you."

Comrade Lengyelova is a good woman, and I am glad for Peti's sake.

Dr. Hurok is in high spirits. "It went off splendidly. It's fortunate that people remember your family. Commissar Lengyelova is an important woman." He gives the same peculiar tilt to the word "important" as Comrade Radek had done.

The square is bathed in sunshine when we walk out of the town hall. Here, alongside this wall, Papa and I were ordered to line up our bicycles and leave them there. I had to leave my brand-new bike tilted against this wall and walk away . . . just like that. "Don't," Papa said, "don't look back. And don't cry. Never look back, only ahead. I promise you, when the war is over, and we'll return with God's help, I'll buy you a new bicycle." I felt his strong hand on my shoulder, and I was not afraid. I stopped crying.

I stopped crying, Papa, because I believed your promise. Papa, you promised me a new bicycle. Where are you, Papa? Why didn't you promise me that you would not be killed and dumped, disfigured, into an unmarked mass grave among nameless, faceless corpses in Bergen-Belsen?

"Everything went off splendidly," Dr. Hurok repeats cheerfully. "Now we must go to the Burial Authority."

CHAPTER FIFTEEN

A Divine Miracle at the Burial Authority

THE COMMISSAR AT THE BURIAL AUTHORITY SPURTS A STRING OF CONSONANTS at Dr. Hurok, her round face impassive. The Slovak language is made up mostly of consonants, but this commissar seems to have forgotten her vowels altogether. I watch and listen with frantic concentration, but am unable to make out a single word that would serve as a clue to what she is saying.

Dr. Hurok looks crestfallen, and during an abrupt pause, he translates: "Comrade Commissar here feels that she needs to consult others in authority in this matter." Dr. Hurok speaks in dispassionate undertones designed to mask his disappointment. "Comrade Commissar believes the unusual nature of our request makes this mandatory. The comrade believes our request requires authorization from the Central Burial Commission. She is referring the matter to Bratislava."

"Bratislava? But that may take weeks, even months. What about the permit from the city commissar, and the others? Don't they count?" I exercise superhuman self-control to contain my terror. I have been made to believe this last step would be a cinch. And now, after everything has gone so well . . .

The telephone rings. The commissar swivels her chair around and talks into the receiver, her back turned to us. Dr. Hurok whispers: "'Referring the matter to Bratislava' means denial."

When the commissar hangs up the phone and swings around to face us, I address her in a desperate last-ditch effort: "Do you speak Hungarian, Comrade?" I ask with affected cheer.

The ruddy-cheeked bureaucrat fixes me with a cold, uncompromising look, then gives an imperceptible nod.

"Comrade, we have every conceivable authorization," I continue in Hungarian. "Here's the permit from the Ministry of Interior in Prague. Here, Comrade Commissar, is the permit of the Health Ministry and the authorization of the Customs Authority in Dunajska Streda. And here, we have just received the permit of the City Commissar of Samorin, signed and countersigned. Comrade Lengyelova herself said that you would be kind enough to issue the Burial Commission's authorization. She assured us that you would help us make proper arrangements for the exhumation. She assured us that you have the sole authority . . ."

The short, stocky woman with a face like a russet apple shakes her head. As she does so, a strand of graying hair slides behind an ear and reveals a distinctive jaw. That jaw joggles my memory. On an impulse I ask, "Comrade Commissar, were you born in Samorin?"

Bafflement registers on the plump face. Her eyes narrow in tandem with the deepening of a wrinkle between them. I cut short her hesitation by blurting out: "What's your name, Comrade?"

"Mihalna," she answers, without removing her puzzled stare from my face.

"But before . . . what was your name before?"

"My name was Posztos."

"Mrs. Posztos was the midwife!"

The russet face drains of color. "But . . . that was many years ago. No one here knows . . . no one knows about that," she whispers in shock.

"Your mother brought me into the world. Irena, don't you recognize me?"

The commissar's eyes and mouth turn into wide-open gaps.

"Don't you recognize me? I'm Elli Friedmann."

The effect is instantaneous. Irena leaps to her feet. "Elli! My Lord, I *do* recognize you!" she shouts, bursting with excitement. "Lord Jesus Christ! You and Marta Mery used to sit in the row behind me. Marta sat right behind me, and you . . . you sat next to her, on the left. Do you remember her? The Merys—Marta and her mother—they live here in Samorin, in the old house. The old lady's still alive, and Marta never married. Elli, where are your braids? Elli Friedmann . . . Lord Jesus, how many years has it been?"

"Thirty-one. And before then . . . we hadn't seen each other for some years before then. How's good Mrs. Posztos?"

"Mother died many years ago," the commissar says, her exuberance suddenly subdued. "No one remembers her anymore."

"Half of Samorin was born at her hands. My mother talks of her often. She remembers the little things Aunt Posztos used to say in order to calm the would-be mother in labor . . . the soft little baby things she used to lay out where the expectant mother could see. A wonderful midwife she was, your mother. She used psychology when no one even knew what psychology was. She used anticipation to allay fears, to soothe the labor pains. Mother remembers her very fondly."

Comrade Mihalna weeps openly.

"Do you want to visit the Merys?" she asks, composing herself, still sniffling. "They live in their old home—it still stands. The Friedmann house is also intact. That street has not been demolished yet. But the Botlos, Molnar, Kovacs, Kovary, Liszt, Sarkozy, Lengyel, and many other families are gone . . . Most of our old friends are gone. Their houses are gone."

"Yes, I know. Comrade Lengyelova told me."

Irena's excitement spills over into a flood of information about what has happened in the intervening years to Samorin, to mutual classmates, neighbors, and to many others, most of them resettled on the "other side." Then, without comment, she sits down at her desk and types out the authorization we'd requested.

Dr. Hurok's mask of official dispassion is thin. In a flash he realizes what is happening, and his face radiates delight. He gives me a surreptitious wink and squeezes my hand.

"You'll need zinc caskets in addition to the regular wooden ones," Commissar Mihalna says, looking up from her typewriter. "As Dr. Hurok here can attest, health regulations require that the bodily remains be sealed in zinc containers before placing them in wooden coffins. I'll see to these things."

She picks up the receiver and spurts rapid monosyllabic consonants, then nods at us.

"Let's go to the storage area. We'll select some wooden caskets, and then the tinsmiths can fit them with zinc containers."

Irena takes a ring of keys from her desk and beckons to us to follow her. "I suggest you buy children's caskets. That's all you'll need. After all these years . . . How many years ago were your grandparents buried?"

"Over fifty."

"After fifty years you'll find only bones, or bone particles, if any. They can easily fit in a child's casket. Child caskets are much cheaper, and their smaller size will cut your shipping costs at least by half. Also, it will make a big difference in the price of the zinc containers. Zinc is expensive," she explains.

Irena picks out two simple caskets and hands them to Dr. Hurok. "These are fine caskets, and reasonably priced," she adds.

Back in the office, the commissar makes out the receipts. Then she summons one of her workers and bids him to accompany us to the tinsmith's, carrying one of the caskets for measure.

"Elli, I suggest you move fast with arrangements. Permits, once issued, may just as quickly be revoked," Irena warns, her voice lowered to a whisper, and I realize she is taking risks in revealing this. I thank her, and she gives me a parting embrace: "Elli, go with God's speed . . ."

Dr. Hurok is incredulous. "This is like a miracle from heaven!" he exclaims as we leave the office. "A divine miracle."

CHAPTER SIXTEEN

The Phantom

THE TINSMITH'S ASSISTANT MEASURES THE CASKETS, AND THEN DECLARES THAT he has no zinc in his workshop.

"How soon can you get it in?" I ask. I am in high spirits in the aftermath of the encounter with Commissar Irena.

"We won't get any in. We don't ever use zinc."

"But we must have zinc for these containers. Where can we get it?"

"Not here. Not anywhere in Samorin. Maybe in Bratislava, but only by governmental order."

"I'm from the Health Ministry," Dr. Hurok interjects. "I can vouch for the legality of this order. You can fill out an application, and I will authorize it."

The young man shrugs his shoulders: "It's up to the supervisor. He's the only one who can write up requisitions."

"Where is your supervisor?" Dr. Hurok asks.

"In Komarno. Comes in only once a month," the young assistant says, and resumes his work. The interview is over.

The sun's oblique rays strike a sheet of white metal propped up against the wall of the smithy.

"What's this?" I ask Dr. Hurok. "Isn't this zinc?"

"It looks like zinc," says Dr. Hurok thoughtfully. He approaches the young tinsmith so he can be heard above the din of soldering. "Young comrade," he addresses the worker ceremoniously. "That sheet of metal outside—it looks like zinc."

"It looks like zinc but it isn't. It's white tin."

"Can you make containers to fit the caskets out of it?" I asked.

"You said you wanted zinc containers," the young man snaps.

I glance at Dr. Hurok. I take the chance: "Dr. Hurok, I have great respect for regulations . . . But, in this case, doesn't it come under a different consideration? After all, we intend to transport human remains, bones that have been buried for over fifty years. There's no fear of contamination here, is there? Perhaps in this case, zinc isn't absolutely essential."

Dr. Hurok examines the shine on his shoes. "I suppose you're right," he says, pausing for a moment without raising his eyes. Then he beckons me to follow him behind the wooden shack. There he whispers: "You must understand, madam. I can't have the customs people finding out that the containers are not made of zinc."

"Okay," I reassure him as I enter the smithy to talk to the tinsmith. "Tell me, Comrade, can a layman tell the difference? If you made the containers out of this tin, would they look like zinc containers?"

"Finished zinc is black."

"Can you paint these black?"

"I can."

"Once painted, would they look like zinc?"

"They would."

Dr. Hurok avoids my eyes as he says, "If they would be finished to look like zinc, I guess it would be all right."

"Thank you, Doctor."

All of the sudden I feel terribly tired. A haze of dizziness descends like a cloud all around me, and it seems as if the smithy is floating, ever so slightly . . .

It is through the haze that I see her approaching. A tall, thin figure wrapped in a large gray shawl, concealing even her face. Her words filter toward me through the woolen fabric and flutter about my head.

"They told me that you . . . that you were here. It is true . . . my God, it is true!" She reaches out with both hands, and her bony fingers close about mine in a tight grip. "I lived to see . . . to meet one of you . . . one of us . . . again."

Who is she? Who is this apparition?

"I didn't want to believe it. They said they saw you in the square. I was sure they were mocking me . . . again. They mock me and call me mad. They all know I have been praying for this day for a long time . . . a very long time. I have been praying to see one of us again, just once more, before I die. And now it's true. You are here . . . You are really here."

Her shaky embrace runs like a shiver through my body. Two silent, silvery lines trickle from her eyes across deep furrows of parched skin onto the thick peasant shawl. The violent shaking of her head seems independent of the fine rhythmic palsy of her frail body.

"Don't you remember me, Elli? I'm Sari Kantor. You must remember my little niece, Evike Lustig. She was your friend. The two of you often played in my backyard, you and Evike, my darling little Evike . . ." Her sobs sputter in short spurts like hiccups. They are little explosive gasps, shrill, childlike.

"And her little brother, Lacika . . . you must remember him. Oh, my God, my dear God." She buries her face in the shawl, and now the entire figure turns into a quaking gray heap. "And my dear brother and his beautiful wife, my sister-in-law—where are they? Where are they all? My family, my friends—what became of them? No one was here when I returned after the war. They were all gone . . . all. And no one told me what became of them. They claimed they didn't know." She raises a tear-stained face and in her eyes I see beyond the pain of loss, bafflement, and the agony of betrayal.

"I had dreamt of the day when I would come home and see them again. And when I came home, they were all gone. You see . . . I . . . you were still a little girl when I left. I married a 'goy,' and my father told me to leave the house. He forbade me to ever step into the house again. I went to live with my husband's family in Bohemia, and waited till I could come home again. I waited in vain. They never even answered my letters—even my dear mother, or brother.

"When I came home after the war, it was too late. They were all gone. I never saw my family again . . ." She wheezes, and her tears flow inwardly, convulsing her body in violent spasms. "But you came back," Sari says. "And now I can die in peace."

She bends down to kiss my hand. I am unable to restrain her. I search for words of comfort, but she silences me with a bony hand raised before her face, now serene.

"No. No. It is as it should be. I deserve no comfort, no eulogies. I have prepared my coffin long ago, and my epitaph for the tombstone. Comrade Mihalna knows it: 'Here lies Sarah the Jewess who deserted her people.' "

The frail body draws erect and the gray shawl ceases its spastic tremor. "God has been kinder than I deserve. I have prayed for this day, to meet one of my people. And now I can die in peace."

Her thin hands draw mine against her wet cheek. "Thank you. Thank you, my child." A teardrop hangs on a parched fold. "God bless you."

She turns to go. Her uneven shuffle is muffled by the soft soil under her feet. I reach out after her but the thin figure in the gray shawl seems to float into the past with dreamlike speed. She is beyond my reach and soon vanishes around the street corner.

Sari Kantor is gone. Had she really been here just a moment ago? The cloud of fatigue is lifting, and I see Dr. Hurok approach.

76

"Madam," Dr. Hurok says, "the gravediggers are under the authority of the Burial Commission. We must speak to Commissar Mihalna about them."

At two o'clock, one of the gravediggers shows up at Irena's office and agrees to do 'the job' on Monday morning. Then Irena introduces me to the hearse driver. "It is up to you to make arrangements for shipment to the Austrian border," Irena advises. Then, lowering her voice, she adds: "It is a deal entirely between the two of you, you and the driver." From her tone I understand that such private "deals" are not altogether legal.

The deal is made, and Tibor the hearse driver agrees that after the exhumation, he will drive us, together with the caskets, to the Austrian border for a fee to be calculated by the kilometer.

All is set for the exhumation on Monday.

I must find a burial society, a *Hevra Kadisha*, to perform the Jewish ritual of the exhumation, a group composed of pious men who have lived moral lives by the precepts of the Torah, reverent of the past and committed to its sanctity. That's the Law. Such men must be the ones to exhume the remains of my grandparents. Their touch will not defile their bones and desecrate their memory.

Where will I find such men by Monday morning?

CHAPTER SEVENTEEN

The Chairman

DR. HUROK BRINGS US BACK TO HIS OFFICE IN DUNAJSKA STREDA IN A HEADY mood of triumph, ready to tell the tale of the miraculous happenings that have occurred. To his surprise, in his office, in addition to Secretary Vrbova and Comrade Radek, there is a stranger in Viola's company.

"This is Comrade Szabados," Viola says, introducing the squat, swarthy fellow with a pencil-thin black mustache and slicked-down black hair as "the chairman of the Culture Committee for this entire region."

"We were fellow freedom fighters," she adds effusively, with obvious pride. "Our association dates back to the antediluvian era—the infant days of the Party."

"The embryo days," Chairman Szabados quips. "Even before the Party's birth!" Then, without waiting for Dr. Hurok to acknowledge his presence, the squat chairman, with grand gestures and considerable pathos, launches into a soliloquy:

"While others were engaged in the pursuit of capitalist gains, selfishly searching for personal and materialistic gratification, we labored to create, formulate, and deliver a Socialist republic, a future of freedom and equality for our people." Turning to Viola, he intones with an expansive chuckle: "Comrade Sternova, here, and myself, we are not only among the Party's parents but also among its midwives . . ."

Comrade Radek, Dr. Hurok, and Comrade Vrbova listen with a show of reverence and dutiful smiles of approval to this litany of self-aggrandizement of this high-ranking Party member. Only Viola's admiration and joy seem genuine.

Samira observes her mother's happy face with a wan smile. She knows Viola the romantic Socialist, for whom these nostalgic moments mean so much. Viola, the product of Czechoslovakia's interbellum liberalism, a Utopian Socialist dreamer, is a rare phenomenon nowadays. She is an old-time Socialist, a prototype who together with her brother Stephan had ever since their early teens lived only for the Cause, and were ready to die for it. Samira's uncle Stephan had volunteered to fight on the Republican side in the Spanish Civil War, and when many others packed up and went home as soon as they discovered it was a lost cause, Stephan remained there, fighting to the bitter end.

In the 1930s, Samira's mother followed in the footsteps of the young Russian Jewish Socialists who had decades earlier escaped from the clutches of the Czarist secret police to Palestine, and there attempted to found a Socialist Utopia. In Tel Aviv, working on the staff of a Yiddish-language Communist newspaper, she met a fellow journalist, and soon the two were married. Little did it matter to the diehard Communist from Czechoslovakia that the young man she loved was an Arab from Lebanon. Their little daughter was three years old when their potential Socialist Utopia became the Jewish State, and Samira's father decided to move his wife and daughter from Tel Aviv to Beirut. To Viola the decision was anathema: As a Communist, why would he prefer Lebanon to Israel? After long, heated debates, Viola's husband admitted that he was an Arab first, and wanted to live among his own people. As such, Viola realized that she had no place in his world.

Samira parted from her father at the Tel Aviv bus station when he boarded a bus bound for Beirut. His departure was the first great trauma of her life. It was the first bitter lesson in the vulnerabilities of an ideal.

When news reached Viola of the Communist takeover of her native Czechoslovakia, all her doubts about the future vanished. In November 1948, the blond, blue-eyed, high-cheekboned Slovak Communist disembarked at the Bratislava Central terminal with her Hebrew-speaking, dark-eyed, dark-haired, half-Arab little girl, in order to present her with a future in the Czechoslovak Communist utopia.

Samira's teeth were cut on Communist ideology. She was the child of a freedom fighter, the elite of the new society, the growing daughter of a high-ranking Party member. She learned Slovak rapidly, forgot Hebrew rapidly, and became a full-fledged member of the Slovak Socialist youth movement. Life held rich promise.

But things changed. Soon her mother was no longer distinguished by honors and, finally, not even invited to important Party functions. In school Samira discovered that she was a Jew. She had suffered from subtle social ostracism all along, but now the epithet *Zhidovka* was openly hurled into her face.

For a long time Samira did not tell her mother about any of this; she sensed Viola's own pain, and although unable to comprehend it, she wished to spare her mother the onus of her own suffering. Then the trauma of 1968 became the watershed of changing realities. Samira's Communism underwent a transformation. Instead of blind faith, she developed a pragmatic acceptance of the system and its foibles. Her credo brought her no joyful elation at festive moments, no bitter disillusionment at times of trial. It did, however, bring her equilibrium. And it was equilibrium that Samira craved most.

As Samira observed her mother's face, filled with joy at the chairman's recollections, Samira's own heart must be filled with sadness for the growing pains Viola still faced.

Viola makes the introductions. When the chairman turns to shake my hand and I find myself face-to-face with him, a sudden sensation of dread reverberates through my body. I know that square face, those piercing eyes . . . Who is this Chairman Szabados?

Comrade Vrbova serves coffee. As I look around the company cozily encircling Dr. Hurok's small desk serving as a coffee table, I think: What a strange *Kaffeeklatsch*! There is Dr. Hurok with his perfectly groomed Vandyke and manners, a vestige of Hungarian flamboyance. Comrade Vrbova, his comely medical secretary. Comrade Radek, the stolid, reliable Slovak bureaucrat. Viola, the white-haired Socialist innocent with dreams intact. And Samira, the pragmatic Palestinian-born Communist bereft of dreams. And here we are, the foreign visitors: Leonard Jackson, the Irish-born Israeli, and myself, the "American," here to extract my family's last remaining roots from my native soil. And there is Chairman Szabados, at the very center, slick and bombastic—the antithesis of the classic Communist freedom fighter. Who is this Chairman Szabados?

The chairman's presence here is an unexpected honor, and the members of the company acknowledge this fact in various ways. Comrade Radek keeps a respectful silence. Dr. Hurok loses his carefree manner, cultivating instead a cautious politeness. He chooses his words carefully and invariably addresses them to the chairman. Vrbova dutifully laughs at his quips. Samira is attentive and thoughtful, and from time to time ventures relevant comments.

Viola is effusive. The chance encounter with such a distinguished old acquaintance who serves as proof positive of her erstwhile prominence makes her giddily happy. She keeps exclaiming: "Can you imagine? After all these years we meet right here on the street, in Dunajska Streda! What a coincidence! We recognized each other instantly, after all these years. By sheer coincidence. I'm grateful to my American friends who provided the opportunity. I came to Dunajska Streda because of them—and ran into my distinguished colleague!"

It is apparent that the chairman is pleased with the warm reception, and he does not hesitate to recall their shared heroic past. Eagerly he offers his own tidbits of memorabilia, the stuff of Czechoslovak Communist history.

He is an ambitious man. The tightly set muscles of his face and the intense fire from his narrow black eyes do little to conceal an appetite for power. An obvious tension between his enormous drive and his stiff self-control sends warning signals into the atmosphere. Who is this man?

The chairman is laughing now, and he displays a wide gap between his two front teeth. Where have I seen this face, this gap between the two front teeth? Where have I heard this laughter?

The exchange of anecdotes climaxes with stories from 1968. An invisible demarcation line keeps you in check. No careless reference breaches the boundary. Even a casual observer can sense the sudden chill that freezes the conversation when "sixty-eight" is inadvertently touched.

But I am no casual observer. I know of the events that made 1968 such a pivotal entity in the lives of these people. I know what Dubcek meant to them. Alexander Dubcek, the homegrown boy who made good. Not only did he put Slovakia on the political map, but he also redrew the Slovak image. The Slovak intelligentsia, for the first time, provided a leader in a liberal cause. Slovak activists played a leading role in overthrowing the Stalinist Novotny regime, and in celebrating the installation of one of their number, Slovakia's favorite son, as president of that liberal oasis in the Eastern Bloc. I know well what Bratislava-born Dubcek as president meant to these Slovak Communists.

Although I lived thousands of miles away, I shared my country-men's anguish when 6,000 Soviet tanks rolled into Czechoslovakia, and crushed not only the nation's freedom but also the Slovaks' personal pride. For these comrades, 1968 was a year of short-lived glory. And the Soviet tanks' crushing their uprising was not only a national defeat but a deep personal trauma, as well. They learned to live with it, in silence.

The world knows that since 1968 the Czechs have been a beaten people. But only insiders know how badly beaten the Slovaks have been. The Slovak Communist Party is a close-knit extended family. Members of the Party are bound by family ties like the Mafia. Even Viola, who had been aware of this, is taken by surprise when Chairman Szabados addresses Dr. Hurok as Stephan and discovers that they are brothers-in-law.

"I'm married to Stephan's sister," the chairman explains. "Dr. Stephan Hurok and I have worked together for years."

"Not exactly together," Dr. Hurok corrects in a somewhat obsequious manner. "Chairman Szabados is my superior. My department in the Health Ministry is under his jurisdiction."

The chairman acknowledges this piece of flattery with a barely perceptible nod.

At this moment, the door opens to reveal a woman standing timidly in the doorway. Her large brown eyes scan the unusual company with childlike hesitancy. Dr. Hurok greets her heartily:

"Enter, Comrade Radekova," he says encouragingly. "Please enter. Let me introduce you to this lovely company. Don't be alarmed. It's not a committee meeting—just a gathering of friends. Come in," he cajoles.

The woman takes a tentative step forward and closes the door behind her.

"Meet Chairman Szabados, Comrade Sternova, Comrade Vrbova, our American guests, and, of course, you know Comrade Radek." Dr. Hurok laughs affably. "Comrades, this is Comrade Radekova, who, I suppose, came in search of a lost husband."

They all laugh except Leonard and Comrade Radekova. Leonard, because he does not understand the remark made in Hungarian, and Comrade Radekova, because she seems overwhelmed as she is moving from one hand to another in the semicircle with painful shyness, acknowledging the introductions with self-conscious handshakes.

"Don't be harsh on him, Comrade Radekova," Dr. Hurok continues his light-hearted banter. "He's been keeping away from you in the line of duty."

The soft features now register a faint smile but the large, brown eyes fill with fear. The mouth slightly tilts to one side revealing a row of perfect teeth. Suddenly I realize that this woman was beautiful—not now, not as a slightly plump matron, but as a young girl, even with a stick-like body, large dreamy eyes glowing in an emaciated face, hair cropped to the scalp . . . and the mouth, tilting to one side in a frightened smile.

"Bonnie?"

As if she'd received an electric shock, Comrade Radekova's head jerks in my direction. Her eyes rivet on my face.

"Bonnie?" I repeat. "Bonnie Koch?"

There is stunned silence in the room.

"Are you Bonnie Koch?"

Fear leaps from the brown eyes: "Who are you?" she murmurs.

"I'm Elli Friedmann, from Samorin. Do you remember?"

Comrade Radekova's eyes engulf her face.

"Do you remember? Auschwitz . . . Plaszow . . . the factory, Michelwerke, in Augsburg? Remember Muhldorf, the Waldlager?"

Comrade Radekova's silence is the silence of the grave. She lowers her eyes. "I remember nothing," she says.

"Are you Bonnie Koch from Kaposvar?"

In total silence a single tear slowly trickles from under an eyelid: "I was."

"Bonnie, you must remember. You must. Please, try—try to remember my mother. You loved her. You called her Aunt Laura. She—"

"Aunt Laura . . ." The woman raises her eyes, and they are dark, brimming pools. "Aunt Laura, from Samorin. Oh, my God . . ."

I open my arms and she flies into my embrace. Tears fill every eye in the room—except those of the chairman. He excuses himself, apologizing; pressing affairs demand his presence elsewhere. In haste he shakes hands all around. When we face each other, now for the second time, and I look into his eyes, I recognize him—and a cold dread grips my insides.

Chairman Szabados is Feri, the eldest son of the town crier in Samorin! I had thought I would never forget Feri Szabados, the young Arrow Cross lieutenant and Gestapo informer during the Nazi occupation. How many Jews had suffered torture and death at the hands of the Gestapo because of rumors supplied by young Szabados? How we, the Jews of Samorin, had feared that square face, those piercing eyes, the famous gap between the two front teeth . . .

I grasp the back of my chair to control my trembling. The room seems to swirl in a vicious dance of vertigo. Is this truly happening? A few moments apart, here in this room, I met a fellow death camp inmate and the Hungarian Nazi who helped make the death camps possible! The Hungarian Nazi, now a high-ranking Slovak Communist!

Revulsion clenches my bowels like icy fingers as Viola is clutching the chairman's hand, beaming an enthusiastic farewell.

CHAPTER EIGHTEEN

Penetrating the Jungle

WE ALSO TAKE OUR LEAVE FROM THE COMPANY AND SET OUT ON THE ROAD. Bonnie and I shake hands. I wonder if we will ever meet again.

Our next stop is the old Jewish cemetery, three kilometers north of Samorin. Viola knows the road to the cemetery, and I carry a mental picture of the graveyard within me—the last farewell at the tombs of my mother's parents.

"I have snapshots of the tombstones," I tell Viola in the car. "Do you want to see them?"

Viola recognizes the light gray marble stone marking my grandfather's grave; she saw it last year. "But the black granite monument lay facedown on your grandmother's grave. I couldn't see the inscription," Viola discloses. "I'm sure we'll find the graves, even so."

As we near Samorin, Viola directs her daughter to turn off the highway onto a dirt road that slices straight across an overgrown field like a knife. Close to the forest, the path narrows and keeps twisting and turning amid wild foliage, thick underbrush encroaching upon the trail and ferociously scraping against the car.

"Stop the car!" Viola yells. "We have to proceed on foot. There is a jungle here. It's impossible to continue by car," she explains as we scramble out of the little Skoda. "Follow me," she yells, and like a diver plunges into the deep thicket. We follow, soon wading chest high in the dense green growth.

Viola is once again the undaunted freedom fighter. She shoves far ahead, undeterred by low-hanging branches and savagely unyielding brush.

At once her voice shoots back from somewhere in the ocean of green: "Watch out!"

I attempt to advance along the narrow path Viola forges in the jungle, but even this seems to vanish, and I have no choice but to lunge blindly in the direction of her voice.

"Watch out, and warn the others!" Her voice rings out again in the green distance. "Soon we are coming to a deep ditch. Careful! Very careful! It's very steep!" She shouts. "You won't see it coming. The grass obliterates the entire ditch. Warn the others behind you!"

As I turn back I can see Len's shoulder, but Samira's hidden from view. I relay the warning and crash on, praying silently. The vegetation now closes in all about me like a tunnel. I have never realized green can be such a frightening color. Again I turn around but this time can see neither Len, nor Samira. Where are they? Have I lost the trail? God, don't let me get lost forever in this green hell . . .

Suddenly a sliver of red flashes among the leaves, and I give a shriek of relief. It is a glimpse of Viola's red T-shirt.

"Anything wrong?" Viola shouts. "Anyone hurt?"

Viola's voice sounds nearer. I have succeeded in narrowing the distance between us!

"Nothing's wrong. But I have not seen Len or Samira for some time."

"Let's wait a few minutes for them to catch up," Viola suggests from somewhere. Now I can hear her breathing heavily, and press ahead in the direction of the sound. My next thrust brings Viola into full view. At that moment she spots Samira's blue tricot top shimmering through the leaves. This is a signal for Viola to crash ahead, without waiting for me to catch up.

Where are we? What actually is the import of hurtling through this prehistoric forest? Why don't we go directly to the cemetery? I cannot remember any woods in the vicinity of the graveyard. On the contrary, I remember well that the cemetery was surrounded by an open vista of flat fields. The woods were several kilometers south, skirting the riverbank.

"Viola, I don't remember any woods near the cemetery," I shout into the thicket. "Why did we come this way?"

"I can't hear you!" Viola's voice drifts through the dense curtain of foliage.

I raise my voice and repeat my question. Viola's laughter rings out: "This *is* the cemetery. We've been in the cemetery all along. Ever since we left the car."

"This—the cemetery? Where's the tall stone fence? And where are the tombstones?"

I remember the high, stone wall that enclosed the cemetery. And the arched metal gate flanked by two ornate stone columns. Within the gate, to the left, there stood a brick structure with black metal doors shut tight, always shut tight.

"What's that house, Mommy, with those black doors?" I'd asked, holding her hand in a tight grip.

"That's the house of the dead," Mother had said matter-of-factly.

Years later, I found out that every Jewish cemetery had a small building where the ceremonial cleansing of the remains in preparation for the burial took place. But back then I'd gulped with panic and gripped Mother's hand tighter. The house of the dead? Did the dead actually live there? I glanced back and prayed for the doors to remain shut—for the dead to stay in their house behind locked doors. That brick house with the black doors remained a symbol of unresolved fear for years to come.

"Viola, where are the gates? And the small brick structure, the house of the dead, near the entrance?"

"There's no fence, no gates, no house of the dead, no entrance.

It's open jungle. Everything was demolished and carted away. Many tombstones were stolen by the local people, and sold. Mostly the granite, the marble, and the other costly gravestones vanished. Lucky my father's and your grandparents' tombs were off the beaten track, obscured by growth. That's how they remained intact," Viola explains as we make our way. "As a matter of fact, there are tombstones all about us, concealed by the brush. If we were to part the branches, they'd reveal rows upon rows, hundreds of graves."

"Look out!" Viola's voice suddenly becomes a shrill alarm. "Hold on to the branches! Here comes the ditch. Warn the others! It's very deep. It's covered by tall grass, so you can't gauge its depth." Now Viola disappears into the ravine, engulfed by the grass rising above her head. "Warn the others! Warn the others!" A disembodied voice rises toward me from below. "They must hold on to the tree branches!"

I wait for Len and Samira to catch up, and pass on Viola's warning. Some of the branches are thick but pliable like heavy ropes, and we hang onto them as we lower ourselves down the steep decline.

From the ravine we emerge into a clearing. Brilliant sunshine shimmers in the green realm. Walking is much easier here, and we advance at a faster pace. Viola halts near a clump of trees and peers among branches she manages to part slightly: "Ah, here it is!"

It takes all four of us to lift a heavy bough that hangs to the ground. One by one we crawl under it and find ourselves in a hidden paradise. Here the brilliant green foliage is splashed with dazzling color. Patches of sunlight vibrate amid yellow, orange, and white flowers; purple berries sprinkle the tops of bushes and myriad insects cavort in a single beam of light.

We proceed to the far end of the grove. All at once Viola points with astonishment: "See that open hole?" she asks. "That was my father's grave. I can't believe it's still open. The gravediggers were supposed to close it right after the exhumation; we paid for extra labor. It is just as it was left a year ago!"

She walks over to the place that had held her father's last remains. "This should not be open. One does not leave a grave uncovered. Even the primitives had customs forbidding it—the open-grave taboo. On Monday, would you ask your gravediggers to throw in a few shovels full of earth? Just so it should not be all open."

"Of course. I'll have them do it."

"And there—there is an elevation, a mound. This must be your grandfather's grave. The marble tombstone is gone! Last year my brother and I brought workers to cut the undergrowth around here so we could get to my father's gravesite. A few trees also had to be cut down. We actually created this grove. It was then that the light gray marble tombstone emerged from the thicket. I read the inscription and became very excited because I knew Uncle Roth, your grandfather. I was about twelve when he died, and my friends and I, all the kids in town, attended his funeral. He was very popular among the kids; he was always nice to us. I was so excited to discover his tombstone. And now it's gone. Had we not cleared this area, it would not have been stolen."

Like a sleepwalker, I approach the overgrown elevation and bend down to part the thick quilt of creepers and run my fingers underneath. Rust-colored clumps of earth crumble between my fingers; a lizard slithers away, and insects scurry deeper into the ground.

An unmarked patch in the wilderness! Is this my grandparents' burial ground?

"I have no doubt this is the spot," Viola says as if reading my thoughts. "The black granite monument was toppled over there. It, too, is gone!" Now Stella points excitedly to a sliver of black shimmering in the grass: "Look, there's a chunk of black!"

"Yes!" Len exclaims, "Here it is." He begins clearing the weeds around the shiny black triangular fragment.

"This is all that's left of the magnificent granite tomb, but at least now we know for sure that this is your late grandmother's gravesite. It also serves as a marker for the lower end of your grandfather's grave."

I sink to the ground and touch the jagged edge of the glistening black stone. Is this it? Have we truly found the graves?

A swarm of insects buzz about me. I smell the cloying aroma of the wet soil. A slow spin has begun . . . the bushes, the trees, the two gentle mounds, the silent hidden graves, all spin in a slow rhythmic sphere around and around. I, too, spin slowly, at one with the whirling jungle—the inexorable, savage green hell.

With trembling fingers I draw from my handbag the photograph of the tombstones taken forty years ago. The black monument is visible behind the gray one, the glossy inscriptions clearly identifying each. I clutch the photograph to my chest and pray silently, and the green fog refuses to dissipate. God, help me. Give me a sign.

"Darling!" Len's voice rings out from the thicket. "I've found something. I found a grave. I'm holding on to an enormous branch, and I can't let go. Can you reach me?"

I rise to my feet and start moving in the direction of Len's voice.

"It's a white gravestone and the cement slab covering the grave is intact. It looks almost like new. Come and look—this way."

Viola and Samira also hear Len and come to help. We reach the spot where Len is gripping a thick tree branch, blood dripping from a gash in his forearm. I can see a white monument wedged between two tree trunks, and I can read Hebrew letters: HANNAH THE WIFE OF . . .

This is the sign. Thank you, my God! How well I knew this gravestone! How many times had I practiced my Hebrew alphabet, deciphering the letters on this stone while Mommy prayed nearby at her parents' gravesite. And when Mommy was done with her prayers, I would help her search for pebbles to place on her parents' graves, and on Hannah Blau's, as well. It was a custom, Mommy explained, a token of respect for the deceased, like a calling card. Mommy would select a nice smooth pebble. "A very fine woman, Mrs. Hannah Blau was," she would say, sighing as she placed a pebble at the foot of her white tomb.

Now the white tomb has emerged from the shadows to give me a divine signal. Like a shaft of light, it looms out of the dark arboreal morass, and I know my search has ended.

I touch the cool ridge of the white gravestone and weep like a child.

CHAPTER NINETEEN

The House in Samorin

"And now, home, sweet home. It's been a long day!" exclaims Viola.

"Would you mind if we drove through Samorin, past our house? It's just a minor detour, I believe. If Samira is not too tired. What do you say?" I ask.

"It's no trouble," Samira hastens to reassure me. "I feel perfectly fine."

"No problem," Viola adds. "No problem at all."

"It's a splendid idea," says Len. "I've been waiting to see your birthplace. Perhaps we can go and see the house itself."

"The house? I'm not sure we can do that. We don't know who lives there now. They don't know me. I don't think we can do that . . ."

No. I don't want to enter the house. I want to drive past, just to see it. It's been such a long time . . . so very long ago. "No, I don't think we should go inside," I say, fear stifling my voice. The others do not respond.

The little Skoda enters Samorin and rolls along sun-drenched streets. I close my eyes; a dull ache drums in my temples. My eyelids are leaden weights. As I force them open. . . there is the corner house. . . there is the acacia tree. The gray house is like a magnet: it draws me nearer and nearer, and I walk in a daze against my will toward the gray house. . Gray? It used to be yellow, like sunshine. The double-winged gate is faded, the paint is peeling in long narrow strips. Where is the bell? There is no bell. Of course . . . there has never been a bell. I knock lightly on the door. There is no answer. What am I doing here in front of this gray house, this faded gate? Only the fragrance of the acacia is familiar . . . but not this house, not this gate.

I knock again, louder.

"Who's there?" A woman's voice, unfamiliar. The language is unfamiliar behind this gate. Slovak. What am I doing here?

"Who's there?" The voice repeats, louder this time.

The sound of the turning key is familiar. The gate flings wide open with a familiar screech. In the entrance, instead of the tall, statuesque woman with fair face and fine features, there stands a short, heavyset woman with a swarthy face and somewhat coarse features. Who is this woman? What is she doing in this doorway?

The fragrance of the acacia is overpowering . . . the sun, blinding. What am I doing here?

"Can I help you, miss?" The woman's eyes wait for an answer.

"I . . . I used to live here. Many years ago."

The face widens into an open smile: "Ah, you've come at last. We wondered when you'd come. Come in, come in."

"No . . . I can't. I'm not alone—my friends are in the car. We're just passing by. We cannot go in."

But suddenly the others are right behind me. The woman with the wide smile holds the door ajar. "Wouldn't you like to come in and see the house?"

I step aside and let the others file through the open gate into the courtyard.

"We've all been waiting for you, miss," the woman says cheerfully. "Ever since your Lady Mother's last letter, old Mrs. Mery talks of nothing else. She told all the neighbors about your coming, and all the neighbors have been waiting for you. This way, please. Come in, miss. Please."

The courtyard is so small, so shabby. Dingy walls, cracked cement, and frayed clothesline. Papa made sure the cement was in perfect repair, the walls gleaming white—and no clothesline. Papa did not allow clotheslines in the courtyard. The courtyard was the entrance hall to the home. It had to be spotless, uncluttered, elegant. "Elegant" was a key word with Papa.

"This way to the kitchen."

What has happened to the kitchen? Where is the ivory wall unit, the gleaming metal range, the fluffy curtains? The fluffy, cream-colored curtains with a thousand ruffles?

A small black stove, pots and pans on open shelves, a rickety table, scruffy wooden chairs, a pile of rags on the floor. What has happened to our kitchen?

A thin man with his feet in a chipped enamel bowl of steaming hot water nods a greeting, and the woman with the wide grin says to him, "Guess who this is?" The thin man with his feet in the enamel bowl, his eyes bewildered, says *Neviem*, which means "I don't know" in Slovak.

The woman scolds in Hungarian: *Beszelj magyarul*—"Speak Hungarian"—and he repeats in Hungarian, *Nem tudom*—"I don't know"—and the woman chuckles aloud.

"It's Young Lady Friedmann, that's who! From America. All the way from America!" she says.

The thin man smiles a tired smile, and nods again, this time awkwardly. He tries to stand up, but cannot. The bottom of the bowl is not wide enough for his feet.

"Fonod's the name," he intones, somewhat abashed.

"Forgive us," the woman says, still grinning. "Forgive my husband. He's just come from work. Forgive his washing up."

"Sorry to intrude. We can come back later."

I must get out. I must get out of here.

Mrs. Fonod will have none of it. She insists on ushering us through the next door. "This is the parlor."

Where's the sofa? Where are the petit-point chairs? The wall tapestry, the carpet, the draperies? A bare wooden table and unpainted wooden chairs, curtainless windows. What have they done to our salon? I must get out of here. But the others are already through the door to the next room, and I follow.

The master bedroom has shrunk. The windows to Main Street are mere peepholes, barely above ground. Why? What's happened to them? And the ceiling is so low. There's no air in here . . . I must get out.

The group is passing through an open door to yet another room. This room is spacious, bright, with curtains on a large picture window, a colorful rug on polished floor.

"What room is this? I don't remember a room here."

Mrs. Fonod's happy, loud chuckle stuns me for a moment: "This used to be your store!"

"The store?"

"Until a year ago it remained as it had been when it was your store. Even the sign that read 'FRIEDMANN GENERAL STORE' above the storefront stayed as we found it twenty-six years ago when the government allocated the house to us. 'You can live in the house as long as you wish,' they told us. 'The owners are gone.' "

Mrs. Fonod's chirpy recollections are razor-sharp blades that slash my insides.

"A year ago our daughter got married," she continues, "and the government gave us a grant to convert the store into an apartment for the young couple. You know how young folks are nowadays. They want everything new. We bought new furniture for them, walled up the storefront, removed the sign . . ." Mrs. Fonod gushes happily. "Look," she says, triumphantly throwing open a door to what used to be our storage room. "Look what we did in here!"

The storage room used to be Papa's exclusive domain. We children were only allowed to enter with permission, even when doing an errand. When the Hungarian Nazis confiscated the store and placed the red governmental seal on the storage room that prevented Papa from entering his domain, something broke inside him. An inner spring snapped, and Papa, the young, dynamic athlete with a keen intellect, became listless and withdrawn.

"Look what we did to the storage room," Mrs. Fonod says again.

My feet are rooted to the ground. I cannot enter the storage room.

"Thank you, no. We must leave now," I say quietly, and turn from the entrance of Papa's storage room, heading toward the exit. "Thank you."

As I pass the kitchen, Mr. Fonod greets me standing on his feet. He's finished his footbath. The others catch up with me on the street, and their faces reflect astonishment. Len lines us all up for a snapshot with Mrs. Fonod near the entrance of the house in Samorin that used to be my home.

As we get into the little Skoda, Mrs. Fonod shouts: "Come back later to share a glass of wine."

A thick cloud of chalk-white dust rises in the air in the wake of the car's sudden lurch forward. I look back but cannot see the faded entrance of the house. I can't even see the acacia tree. A blanket of dust obliterates the entire view of the town.

CHAPTER TWENTY

Papa's Castle

APRIL 1944

A THICK HAZE OF DUST OBLITERATES MY LAST LOOK AT OUR HOME. THE WHITE dust blankets everything—the house, the acacia tree, the entire green hill on the corner. Will I ever see my home again? Will I ever sit under my beloved tree on the hill? Will I ever run on the sun-blanched dirt road all the way to school?

The cart picks up speed and now the dust cloud swallows the whole town.

"I cannot see anything," I call to Mother, who sits next to the coachman. "I wanted to watch as long as I could, but there's too much dust."

"Stop torturing yourself. Come, sit here, and face the road. Come."

I clamber to the front seat, and now I can see the cart ahead of us piled high with some of our furniture. The police allowed us to take along one roomful of things. Papa is sitting on that cart. I can barely see him; all that stuff blocks my view. Poor Papa . . . how he hated to get on that rickety cart, to leave our house behind, with all our things disheveled. Silent and pale, he walked slowly out of the house he loved, the home he was so proud of . . . perhaps forever. My home is my castle, he used to say. As long as we're in our castle, no harm can come to us, he declared.

And now he'd been forced to leave his castle and sit on that shaky peasant cart that is taking us farther and farther away. His stiff, proud posture belies his humiliation, the last shred of pride stripped from him. Oh, Papa, don't make my heart ache for you so.

"That's a good girl," Mother says. "Sit next to me, and look ahead. Remember, my little girl: Never look back! Look only ahead. Wherever we go, always look ahead. Wherever we go, as long as we're together, that place will be our home."

CHAPTER TWENTY-ONE

Gone Is the Jewish Quarter

ON THE ROAD BACK TO BRATISLAVA, MOTHER AND DAUGHTER ARE IN AN ELATED mood. They are chatting happily in the front seat. Len and I listen in silence. I am bone-weary, and Len, as usual, has absorbed my feelings as if by osmosis.

Perhaps this is the right moment to inform our hostesses that we wish to move to a hotel. In her correspondence Viola had offered to share her home for the duration of our stay in Czechoslovakia, and, fully aware that Europeans consider it an affront when a visitor elects hotel residence over homegrown hospitality, I accepted.

We, however, find it awkward to impose on the two women's privacy. We know that we are displacing Samira from her sleeping place on the living room couch, causing her to sleep on a narrow cot in a small storage nook. We are sorry to clutter up the meticulous living room with our luggage.

There is also the matter of food. Viola and Samira do not have a kosher kitchen, and we are concerned that our strict observance of dietary laws may be misinterpreted as aloofness on our part. Len and I are prepared to live on bread, sardines, vegetables, and beer as we did in Vienna, but this entails the privacy a hotel room provides.

I broach the subject carefully, and Viola, in her expansive mood, takes no offense. I also tell her that in New York we received the addresses of two widows, Mrs. Erber and Mrs. Kahn, who on occasion cooked kosher meals for visitors from abroad.

"Perhaps we can contact them," I suggest, "and see what arrangements can be made, especially for the Sabbath meals."

Viola is glad to help us find these two widows. "Perhaps they have telephones," she says. "In Bratislava nowadays, most people have a telephone," she reassures us.

I am relieved that both the subject of the food and the hotel is settled with ease. It is agreed that Len and I will move to the Hotel Carlton on the Danube bank tomorrow morning.

"The Carlton—ah, yes!" Viola voices her approval with enthusiasm. "An old hotel, a Bratislava landmark—and not too far from us. You won't even need a taxi. It's about five minutes from our flat."

As soon as we reach home, Viola sets about locating the two widows. Although they are not listed in the directory, she finds their numbers by contacting mutual acquaintances.

I call Mrs. Erber first and introduce myself in Hungarian, explaining that my husband and I wished to have our Sabbath meals at her place, if possible.

"It is Thursday evening, and I understand this is short notice," I say apologetically. "Would you be able to accommodate us?" I ask, assuring her that I would understand if she declined.

There is a long silence on the line. Then a suspicious, almost hostile voice inquires about my name, my whereabouts, and the name of the person who gave me her phone number. I repeat my initial introduction and explanations. Even after mentioning the name of the New York friend who recommended her cooking, Mrs. Erber remains cold, hesitant.

"It's a mistake," she says curtly. "I know nothing about kosher meals."

I am baffled and disappointed. That leaves bread, beer, and sardines.

"Can you at least tell me where can we pick up bread for the Sabbath? I mean the traditional braided *challah*."

"There's no *challah* for sale in Bratislava," she says, and then, to my great surprise, she volunteers to bake two loaves of *challah* for us.

"You must pick them up in person," she warns. "Tomorrow morning. Early."

I thank her happily and promise to be at her home, number 5 Nesporova Ulica, bright and early tomorrow morning.

Then I call the second widow, Mrs. Kahn. She is friendlier, but just as elusive about kosher food as Mrs. Erber.

"I cannot discuss it over the telephone," she snaps. "Can you come to my place, number 5, Nesporova Ulica, tomorrow morning? We can talk in person."

Same excuse. Same address. Same time. Are these two women twins?

Then I remember: 5 Nesporova, formerly, Svoradova, a tall gray building, used to be one of the Jewish community buildings, housing the rabbi, the ritual slaughterer, the teacher, and other community servants. I was told that Mrs. Erber was the widow of the former rabbi, and Mrs. Kahn, of the Jewish teacher. Perhaps 5 Nesporova still housed Jewish civil servants.

Viola is also puzzled by the mystery surrounding kosher food. Samira feels the women must have a good reason, and she's very curious to find out what that reason is. Len and I promise to investigate and let her know what we find out.

I'm looking forward to my appointments at Nesporova Ulica with fond anticipation. Nesporova Ulica 7 was a dormitory for girls, and my home after the war for more than two years.

All at once the memory of dread shatters my happy thoughts as I think of the building that is adjacent to the girls' home—Nesporova

9. The tall, impressive building was the Catholic Seminary—and oh, how the seminarians had hated us Jewish girls, young survivors of the Holocaust. Even today, how vulnerable I am to the memory of that hatred. I can still feel the terror they instilled in our hearts, even after all these years.

Len and I start out on foot before 8:00 AM, heading toward Nesporova Ulica. It is a somewhat cool, sunny morning, and the wisps of breeze from the Danube slap moist patches of air against our faces. Len shares my excitement; his face is flushed and a boyish sparkle lights up his deep brown eyes.

We reach the square with the Slovak poet's statue at its center in ten minutes. From here it's less than twenty minutes to the Jewish Quarter. The narrow cobblestone alley on the right winds its way uphill past pocket-sized parks and tiny water fountains. A sharp turn, so narrow you almost brush both sides of the alley with your shoulders at the same time, reveals the Wide Stairs. My heart gives a jolt. The familiar jagged old stairs worn to a bright pink polish stretch out before us! How intimidated I was by these steep stairs as a small child, when Mommy vigorously bounded up them with me, a little village girl unfamiliar with stairs, in tow. They filled me with awe as I climbed higher and higher, delighting in the brilliant shine of the pink stone they were made of.

"One must climb these stairs to Michalovska Street," I say to Len. "Michalovska leads to the Judenstrasse, the Jew Street."

The Royal Castle towered right above Jew Street, a symbol of power and authority, and protection for Jewish subjects, commanding the view of the Danube and the hills. Jewish subjects paid heavily for this privileged location at the foot of the Castle. The Jew tax flowed directly into the coffers of the Castle dwellers. It was protection money. Blood money. Sometimes it provided protection from persecution and attack, and sometimes it did not. And when it did not, the cobblestones of Jew Street ran with Jewish blood.

We climb the wide stairs.

"On top of the stairs is Michalovska. There we'll turn left to Edlova. From there, we'll reach Jew Street in a matter of minutes," I explain to Len with happy anticipation. "From the corner of Edlova we'll get an excellent view of Jew Street snaking downward to the Danube and flanked by schools, handsome synagogues, yeshivas. We will see the magnificent cupola of the Neologue Temple with its Romanesque splendor, the intricate Gothic structure of the Ortho-dox Synagogue, the massive building of the yeshiva which my brother attended as a young boy . . ."

All at once, out of nowhere, metal barriers spring up and put a stop to our advance. A deep, dark canyon stretches below our feet, a deep, wide chasm that extends from Castle Hill all the way down to the riv-erbank! What has happened? Has a volcanic eruption ripped open the belly of the city, plunging the entire Jewish Quarter into the primordial abyss? Has the bottom fallen out from under Jew Street, causing it to tumble without a trace into the jaws of this bottomless void—cupolas, Gothic and Romanesque structures, spiral staircases? When did this happen? How? I gape, speechless, at the terrifying sight.

I grip the metal barrier and close my eyes. Perhaps by some magic it will all reappear by the time I open them again—the lively street with its spectacular structures; the people, young students and their teachers, mothers with baby carriages, men, women in their Sabbath best, hurrying to the synagogue . . . By what madness do I expect to conjure up the past?

"Strange," Len says slowly. "Viola did not mention anything about the disappearance of the Jewish Quarter. I wonder when this hap-pened, and why?"

From the Edlova intersection we can see the far end of the canyon narrow into a tunnel near the Danube, where tiny Skodas and Tatras rush in a steady stream, and a modern highway rises in an arch above.

Len exclaims: "Look! That's the new bridge that we crossed on our way here from Vienna!"

I take Len's arm and we retrace our steps to the next intersection. There a passerby directs us to Nesporova Ulica in a roundabout way.

"Let's go to number 7 Nesporova first—to the dormitory where I lived after the war."

I walk up the familiar stairs and ring the bell. A sign on the door says POLICE STATION, DISTRICT 4. There is no answer.

Len finds a narrow gate in the wire fence that flanks the building, and opens it. I follow him on the thin path among the weeds till we reach the backyard. How small it is! How did we, eighty-five girls, find room in this small yard to dance the *hora* around the campfire night after night, singing *Eretz Israel, nasha sveta zem*—Land of Israel, our sacred Land . . .

I raise my eyes and see the windows of the tall, adjacent building towering above the yard. The Svoradov Catholic Seminary. Those windows up there were filled with faces when we danced—laughing, jeering faces. The faces emitted abusive sounds when we danced and sang, and sometimes buckets of water came tumbling from the windows, sometimes rocks. From high above, from the tall windows of Svoradov Catholic Seminary, the splashing buckets of water extinguished our campfires.

And the girls, survivors of Nazi brutality, retaliated by building another campfire, and another, singing even louder, dancing even with more spirit.

On a cold, damp November night, the girls danced and sang longer than ever, and the campfire was larger than ever. It was the night the United Nations voted to let the Jews have their Promised Land. And our song, our dance, was an open declaration of triumph, of thanksgiving.

That night the seminarians, instead of hurling insults, or water, or rocks from high above, came to our yard with buckets and sticks. From the buckets they splashed a foul-smelling liquid at us girls and at our campfire, and their sticks struck at our shoulders, heads, arms, and legs. They swung their sticks without even looking, wildly, ferociously, cursing and laughing. The girls shrieked with fright and the campfire became a smoldering heap.

The bruises on our bodies healed slowly. The bruises on our souls perhaps never healed.

The windows of the tall building are mute now, and a blanket of weeds buries the drama that took place in this yard.

———— • ————

I follow Len out of the yard, and we go next door, to Nesporova 5, to pick up our *challah* from Mrs. Erber. A hand-lettered sign— MRS. HANNAH ERBER—marks the door. A slim woman, her hair tucked under a faded scarf, opens the door and wordlessly ushers us into the apartment. She hurriedly wipes her hands on a worn apron and extends her right with awkward formality, saying, "Hannah Erber."

I introduce Len and myself, adding that my husband speaks neither Slovak nor Hungarian. Our appearance seems to inspire confidence. Mrs. Erber's gray eyes fix on my face openly: "Forgive me," she says softly. "You see, I couldn't tell you over the phone, but there is no kosher meat in Bratislava, and that's why I couldn't invite you for meals on the Sabbath. We three widows are the only ones who eat kosher in Bratislava. We sometimes travel to Budapest to buy kosher meat, and smuggle it in. It's . . . it's not legal, you understand. We bring small pieces hidden in our handbags, or on our bodies." She lowers her eyes. "It's quite risky."

She smoothes the folds of her apron, and, lowering her voice even more, continues: "I haven't been to Budapest for a while. I hope you'll forgive me."

Suddenly, she blushes: "The *challah*! I almost forgot!" She hurries out of the room and returns with a small package wrapped in crumpled brown paper.

"What do you prepare for the Sabbath meals?"

"It's no problem, really. On Wednesday there were carrots at the market. And today they brought in green peppers. Potatoes I have from last week. But for guests . . . guests should have a proper meal on the Sabbath."

I thank her for the *challah*. She accepts the proffered bills eagerly, tucking them with an embarrassed blush into the pocket of her apron.

Mrs. Kahn and her home present a contrast. She is short and rotund, and her house is bright and airy. As soon as we are seated, Mrs. Kahn hurriedly closes the windows, draws the curtains, and in a whisper repeats the tale of kosher meat we have just heard from Hannah Erber.

Mrs. Kahn, however, has good news. Three days ago an unexpected visitor from Budapest brought her two kilos of meat. "I was going to save it for the High Holidays, but after your phone call I removed it from the freezer, and it's already boiling merrily on the stove. The Sabbath is fortunate this week, and it's to the merit of our esteemed visitors from America," she says with a bright smile.

At this moment I realize the depth of the abyss that has swallowed up Jewish life in this once prominent royal capital, and my heart fills with more pain.

CHAPTER TWENTY-TWO

A Teenager's Dream

It is almost noon when we return to Viola's to pack our things for the move to the Carlton Hotel. Samira is at work, but Viola helps us carry our luggage to the elevator and down to the waiting taxi.

Moving into this grand old hotel is a teenager's dream come true. I was fifteen when I made myself a promise that one day I would be a guest at this hotel, in the company of a handsome, suave man, just like Mr. Mikus.

Mr. Mikus, our neighbor from across the street, used to offer me a ride in his sports car to Bratislava whenever he drove there on business. It was the postwar period, and the Russian occupiers were still in the country. Most stores were still closed; buses and trains were not running. There was no public transport to Bratislava, where my brother Bubi was a university student. As food was scarce, Mom would grasp at every chance to send him provisions, and it was my task to deliver the food parcels. Most often I would hitch rides to the city in other neighbors' horse-drawn carriages.

But the ride in Mr. Mikus's sports car was the highlight of my week. The most exciting part of the trip was our meeting for the ride home at the Café Carlton in the hotel lobby. Mr. Mikus, a distinguished-looking man in his early forties, would sit at one of the round tables of the café, sipping cappuccino and scanning the evening newspapers. As I approached he would rise and invite me to join him. I'd politely decline, and Mr. Mikus would finish his cup, fold the newspaper, and ask the liveried attendant to deliver his car to the hotel entrance.

Café Carlton was the glamour spot of postwar Bratislava. Here the city's intellectuals and artists strove to recapture the ambience of the prewar Republic. In cozy little corners they sipped cappuccino, espresso, or mocha from tiny Rosenthal china cups and smoked cigarettes in long silver holders. The Café Carlton was an island of sophistication and color, where romantic music mingled with sparkling wit, elegant women flashed expensive jewelry—a brief flare-up of prewar brilliance—a dramatic finale before the brutal descent of the Iron Curtain. Mr. Mikus introduced me to this dazzling world of glamour, and it left me with a lingering nostalgia.

For me, the return trip to Samorin, the wintry scene of bare trees and stark houses on the roadside, was transfused with the glow sparked by the fleeting glimpse into the world of Café Carlton. From my first exposure to that world, Samorin became a waiting room for the periodic trip to Bratislava with Mr. Mikus.

On one occasion I wore a new dress. It was a brown woolen dress with turquoise trimming, a flared skirt, and a wide patent-leather belt. It had arrived in a CARE package from America. When Mom and I unfolded it, we noticed a large ugly hole, a round cigarette burn, on the front of the skirt.

"What a shame!" Mom exclaimed. "This unsightly cigarette burn ruins the dress."

"How lucky for us," I countered. "Thanks to that cigarette burn, the owner donated it to CARE! If not for that unsightly hole she would still be wearing this dress, and we wouldn't be its lucky recipients!"

Mother laughed out loud. "How right you are! Smart girl," she praised, then added: "I'm happy you're able to see the bright side of things."

Mom's skillful fingers quickly remodeled the dress, cleverly hiding the hole, and I had an elegant new dress—my first new dress since we'd returned from the death camps. Up till then I'd worn the dress I had been given in Concentration Camp Augsburg in the winter of 1944. The shipment of dresses came to us from Auschwitz, and in my dress I discovered the name of the young girl to whom it had belonged, stitched into a hidden seam of the dress. It became my dress of torment, as I knew it had been stripped off her body in the gas chamber. For almost two years I wore that dress, and the agony did not diminish with the passage of time.

Now the CARE package had liberated me from that burden. It gave me a new life. I was no longer an inmate of a death camp. I was like everyone else. I wore a dress that was just a dress—not a garment of agony.

The new dress transformed me. I became a grown-up in that dress. The elegant cut flattered my height and lanky shape, and the rich brown fabric accentuated my light blond hair and green eyes. I was no longer a scrawny fifteen-year-old girl; I had become an elegant young woman. The effect startled us both. Mom and I looked at each other and embraced, overwhelmed by the joy and the pain of a new life.

I persuaded Mom to let me wear the new dress for my next trip to Bratislava. At the end of the day, as I went to meet Mr. Mikus in the lobby of the Carlton Hotel, the attendant removed my coat and I walked into the café in my new dress. Mr. Mikus looked up from his paper, sprang to his feet, and made a deep bow. This time he did not accept my refusal to join him for a cup of cappuccino. I blushed as the waiter ceremoniously placed the delicate china cup and saucer in front of me with a bow.

This was the first time in my life that I'd tasted the delightful bitter drink, and I sipped slowly, daintily, as did the elegant women at the other tables. My head was spinning a little, and I felt all eyes upon me. My heart was brimming with bliss. I was in love with Mr. Mikus and the world. I was in love with being a woman.

Later, when we were in the car, Mr. Mikus said, "I have an idea. Would you graciously consent to do me a favor? It's an unusual one, and I must ask your forgiveness. But tonight you look so strikingly like someone I know, a friend, that I thought I would ask you . . . Would do me a favor and try on . . . a present that I've been planning to buy for her as a surprise? You're the same height, the same build, the same coloring. If it looks good on you, I'm sure it would look good on her. I've never before noticed the striking resemblance between the two of you. Do you mind?"

I could barely conceal my excitement. Mr. Mikus's affairs were the stuff of whispered gossip in Samorin. Beautiful dancers, celebrated singers, actresses . . . Poor Mrs. Mikus had long resigned herself to Joska's affairs. He was a good man and he loved his family. But he was also an attractive man of the world, and she was a small-town, overweight "little goose." "Little Goose" was his pet name for her, and Maria Mikus had accepted her role.

Of course, no one had "witnessed" any of Mr. Mikus's affairs; it was all rumor. No one from Samorin was fortunate enough to have met him in the company of his glamorous girlfriends. They had only heard about them, and were intrigued, weaving colorful tales of his exploits. Now I was to be initiated into Mr. Mikus's secret world! I was excited, and flattered that he'd chosen to confide in me.

"Of course I don't mind. I'm delighted to oblige," I said in a low voice, pretending to sound nonchalant.

"Thank you," Mr. Mikus said with an engaging smile. I felt he considered me an equal.

He parked the car in front of a fashionable fur salon. Then he escorted me through the carpeted foyer into the elegant showroom, complete with pastel-colored rugs, petit-point *fauteuils*, and crystal chandeliers. A white-gloved attendant removed my threadbare winter coat and carried it with a flourish to a gilded rack nearby. There it hung among cashmeres and furs, a source of acute embarrassment for me.

I was seated in one of the cushioned armchairs when the salesman appeared with several fur coats draped on his arm. When he reached me, he bowed and smiled expectantly. Mr. Mikus selected a dark-brown long-haired fur and asked me to try it on. I rose to my feet and the salesman helped me slip into the soft coat, then buttoned it to the top of the high collar.

I felt like a pampered kitten, warm, cozy, and sheltered. What a luxurious feeling! I walked with care, slowly, as if dancing on air. The look on Mr. Mikus's face made my heart beat faster and my throat constrict. He did not speak for a few seconds; then, he asked me to step before the mirror. I did not recognize myself! Before me stood a woman, demure and elegant, like a model on the cover of a fashion magazine. This was not I. This was not the adolescent whose starvation sores had only recently healed, who only yesterday still wore the dress from Auschwitz. This was someone else. This was a striking woman in a most beautiful fur coat. The long, silky, darkly gleaming fur made me look even taller and fairer.

"How do you like it?" Mr. Mikus's voice was constrained.

"It's . . . it's lovely. A lovely coat."

"You are lovely . . ."

I blushed, and swallowed hard.

Mr. Mikus turned to the salesman. "We're taking it."

The salesman produced an enormous box and placed the coat into the box among sheets of tissue paper with great care.

In the car Mr. Mikus began in a solemn voice: "I wish to thank you, and tell you . . . ask you . . . would you like to meet my lady friend? We could drive over to her place right now and surprise her. What do you say, Ellike? I'd like you to meet her. You'll be struck by the resemblance."

I was astonished. Was he serious? Was he going to introduce his latest inamorata to me? Was I going to meet one of those mythical celebrities face-to-face? Did he trust me to such an extent?

"Well? What do you say, Elli? Perhaps you'd rather not?"

"Oh no, no, no. I'd be glad . . . happy to meet her. Who is she?"

"She's an actress, onstage, at the National Theater. She's a very beautiful lady, and a very good actress. You'll like her. It'll take just a few minutes. All I want is to deliver the coat, and we'll be on our way. But if you'd rather not, I can have the coat sent and we can drive straight home."

"Oh, no, no. I *do*. I *do* want to meet her."

"Thank you, Elli. Her name is Vrenka . . . Vrenka Kapucinska."

Vrenka Kapucinska lived in a small villa on the Palisades, an exclusive part of the city. Her maid opened the door, evidently surprised at seeing Mr. Mikus in the company of a young girl. She eyed me suspiciously, so Mr. Mikus introduced me as his son Imre's friend. The maid ushered us into the salon, a quaint room furnished in Chinese Empire style with Oriental wall hangings and silk scrolls. I had never seen anything like it.

My wide-eyed fascination with the furnishings did not last long. Madame Vrenka entered the room. She was a statuesque woman with light blond hair piled high on her head. Her eyebrows, penciled lines, arched above eyes that were gigantic and green, like an Egyptian cat's, now focusing on Mr. Mikus and the enormous box in his hand. The carefully painted face broke into a wide smile: "My darling Joska," she exclaimed. "What a surprise!"

"This is Miss Friedmann, our young neighbor, Imre's friend. She graciously consented to try this on so I could surprise you. Voilà!" Mr. Mikus opened the box and let it drop on the carpet, raising high the fur coat in one hand. Vrenka's eyes turned into two green saucers with excitement. She flew into his arms.

"Joska, you're an angel!"

Mr. Mikus helped her into the coat, and Madame Vrenka ran to the full-length mirror in the corner. It, too, was Empire style, and the tall blonde looked incongruous against its dark, delicate Oriental frame.

"Joska, *mily moj* . . . my love! It's beautiful. It's breathtakingly beautiful! Thank you." She walked over to Mr. Mikus and gave him a kiss on the cheek. Then she turned to me, and extended her hand: "Thank you, for being so kind."

Madame Vrenka was a gracious, beautiful woman; the coat fitted her magnificently. I did not understand how Mr. Mikus could have compared me to her. Could I ever grow up to be so beautiful?

It was getting late, and Mr. Mikus apologized. We had to leave at once.

In the car he was chattier than usual.

"You looked stunning in that coat," he remarked. "One day, when you're older, someone will buy you such a coat. A very lucky man."

I was staggered by the remark. I did not know what to say. We drove home in silence. I expected Mr. Mikus to ask that the little episode be kept secret, but he did not say anything. Had he taken for granted that I would be discreet without being warned? Did he trust me so implicitly that such a warning was superfluous? Was there an understanding between us?

The car came to a stop in front of our house. Mr. Mikus swiftly appeared at the passenger door and held it open, then reached for my hand to help me step out of the car. He had never done that before.

We had arrived at my home, but something had changed. This was not the same street. These were not the same houses. They were different, somehow. Everything was different. Everything was cloaked in a soft haze, as if wrapped in a cloud of magic. I was fifteen, but I was a woman in love with the future.

One day a handsome man would hold my arm as I stepped out of his car, and he would lead me up the carpeted stairs of the Carlton Hotel.

CHAPTER TWENTY-THREE

A Memorable Meal

OUR ROOM AT THE CARLTON HOTEL LIVES UP TO MY ROMANTIC EXPECTATIONS. I revel in the frilly curtains that flank the intricately carved window frames; the elaborate Louis XIV furniture; the richly ruffled bedspreads, in matching bone color; the dark red carpet; and the rococo lampshades.

I place a long-distance call to Herr Handler in Vienna, informing him of Monday's imminent exhumation. Herr Handler is the Viennese travel agent we'd contracted to handle the shipment of the caskets at the Austrian end. I also call Irena at the Burial Commission to remind her of the appointment, and to double-check whether the gravediggers, hearse driver, and tinsmiths were aware of the date and time of the exhumation. The customs officer had to be reminded as well. Mr. Radek has volunteered to serve as the health supervisor at the gravesite, and I give him a call as well before the Sabbath.

In one corner of our room there is a small refrigerator, a nod to progress. We had done some grocery shopping and fully expected that we'd have to keep the butter in a sink full of cold water, our fruit and vegetables on the windowsill. Instead, what modern luxury— twentieth-century convenience in the midst of eighteenth-century extravagance!

I quickly plug in the refrigerator so that by the time we finish unpacking, it will be cool enough to store the foodstuffs.

Enormous closets swallow up all our belongings: no more dressing in and out of suitcases in the middle of a living room. We delight in the convenience of a bathroom with running hot water. We had neither bathed nor showered since Vienna. In Viola's apartment hot water ran only on Thursdays, but this Thursday must have been an exception: There was no hot water, and the two women patiently explained that this was rather unusual. They were certain that there would be hot water next Thursday.

An hour later the beer in the refrigerator is still warm. Len checks the butter; it is soft. I call Reception immediately, but the operator knows neither German nor Hungarian.

"Only Slovak, please—*prosim*."

Out of sheer desperation, the Slovak word for "refrigerator" springs into my head. "*Hladnica!*" I exclaim with relief, and then the words *ne robotit*—does not work—slide out as if by magic.

I am stunned. How mysterious are the workings of the human brain! There are untold cells in the brain, waiting dormant sometimes for decades, only to be reawakened at the right moment. I had not spoken Slovak for over three decades, and believed I had forgotten it altogether. Throughout the years of non-use, the language had dropped out of my awareness, and now, because of need, entire sentences have popped into my mind, catching me unawares. How wonderful!

The operator is happy to have understood me, and she promises to attend to the matter immediately. Within seconds, there is a knock on the door; it is the technician, and within minutes the little icebox is purring like a contented kitten.

I cover the small table with a white linen towel, glue two candles into the crystal ashtray, cover the *challahs* with a white table napkin, and light the candles for the Sabbath. As we walk to our dinner appointment at Mrs. Katz's home in Nesporova Street, darkness settles over the silent streets. A pale moon is suspended above the city, casting an eerie light on the ramp, the railings, and the road signs; then, suddenly, darkness swallows all.

There are no streetlights, and when we reach Nesporova we wander uncertainly in the pitch-black street. Which one of these buildings is number 5? Suddenly, a disembodied voice rings out through an open window: "*Shabbat Shalom!*" We recognize Mrs. Katz's voice, and we follow it into the building.

By contrast, the dining room is an oasis of light. A six-branched silver candelabra with six tall candles stands in the middle of the large table, covered with a white damask tablecloth. A large silver goblet filled to the brim with red wine is surrounded by an assorted array of smaller silver goblets. Besides Mrs. Katz, there are two elderly matrons at the table. All three stand up as we enter, and greet us with a hearty *Shabbat Shalom*.

Mrs. Katz does not stand on ceremony. Without introducing the other two guests, she hurriedly hands Len the full goblet of wine and urges him to recite the *Kiddush,* the benediction over wine—the ceremonial opening of the Sabbath meal.

"Thank you, Mrs. Katz," mumbles Len in barely audible tones, conscious of the language barrier. He takes the goblet and begins to chant a song, welcoming the Sabbath. The ice is broken; the ladies join in, their eyes sparkling, faces glowing with the thrill of the spirited melody, and the room fills with the bliss of Sabbath. With Len's recitation of the *Kiddush* and his distribution of the wine into the goblet of every person around the table, the festive mood reaches a climax.

Even before her guests are seated, Mrs. Katz appears with steaming bowls of yellow soup weighed down by heaps of thin pasta. As soon as the bowls have been placed before us, Mrs. Katz begins to eat, advising all to follow suit. "Hurry—the soup will get cold," she urges between lusty slurps. The company obeys without protest, and the air fills with the symphony of slurping.

As soon as the soup bowls are empty Mrs. Katz snatches them, darts into the kitchen, and almost instantaneously reappears with a tray of plates, each heaped with small chicken parts and piles of non-descript yellow mush. She places a dish in front of each guest, and once again issues a firm exhortation to begin eating right away. The chicken bits are quite tasty, but the yellow stuff is too sweet, and I know that Len will not be able to eat it. He hates anything sweet. I recognize the dish as squash prepared with sugar and vinegar. Poor gallant Len is forcing himself to eat in order not to offend the hostess. I had seen him on other occasions suffer through abominable dishes in deference to the hostess's feelings. Now I steal a glance at him and see his face exude utter despair; the wine is objectionable to him, as well. It is sweet Israeli wine.

I ask Mrs. Katz in Hungarian whether she has some Hungarian table wine.

"Of course, but I would not serve it to honored guests from Israel," she announces proudly. "For this occasion I opened a bottle of imported wine from the Holy Land, the sweet nectar of the sacred soil."

The problem is solved when I apply some tactful, diplomatic coaxing, and Mrs. Katz produces a bottle of dry Hungarian wine. Len's mood changes radically; now at least he is able to wash down the cloying sweetness of the squash preparation with a "civilized" drink.

By the end of the dinner Mrs. Katz gets around to the introductions. One of the two ladies is a visitor from New York, a native of Bratislava who has come to pray at her parents' graves in the local Jewish cemetery. The other one is a remarkably youthful eighty-five-year-old widow, also a native of Bratislava, who lives in the building and regularly joins Mrs. Katz for Sabbath meals.

As it turns out, in addition to Hungarian, all three women speak German and some English, so the conversation flows quite freely. It focuses on life stories, and, as usual, each personal tale is a minute tile in the mosaic of the Jewish historical narrative.

The visitor from New York, Mrs. Lowenthal, fought with the Slovak partisans during the war, and fled to the United States after the violent Communist takeover of her homeland. The octogenarian, Mrs. Vrba, escaped to Shanghai via Siberia after her son's arrest by the "Hlinka Guards" during the Nazi era, then lived in Australia for years, returning here only after her husband's passing. Mrs. Katz, a survivor of the concentration camps, did not return to her native Hungary when she found out that her family had perished in the Holocaust, and her only surviving sister settled in Dublin. On her way to join her sister, she tarried in Bratislava long enough to meet and marry a local boy who then served as the city's rabbi.

Irish-born Len, whose grandfather had escaped from Czarist Russia, went to Israel via England, in whose army he had served in India during Word War II, and via Canada, where he'd practiced medicine for two decades. A native of this region, I went to live in Israel after an odyssey in Polish and German concentration and displaced person camps, and a twenty-five-year sojourn in the United States.

———·◆·———

The streets are dark and forbidding when we make our way back to the hotel. The moon is hiding behind thick clouds, and the streetlights are too scanty to provide adequate light. The hotel lobby is also deserted and dimly lit. Our two Sabbath candles still flicker in the bathtub.

On Sabbath morning we rise early in order to reach the synagogue in time for services. Viola had explained that there was only one house of Jewish worship in Bratislava that was open for services on Sabbath, and it was far from the Carlton.

CHAPTER TWENTY-FOUR

The Informer

BRIGHT SUNSHINE FLOODS THE STREETS AS WE HEAD TOWARD THE SYNAGOGUE.
Along the way we pass some enormous department stores and the
famous Manderla building, Bratislava's eleven-story "skyscraper." The
streets are alive with traffic, and the sidewalks, with pedestrians.

Finally we reach the synagogue on Heydukova Street, a stately
structure with a graceful portico. The synagogue's spacious interior
is dark and hollow. A handful of worshippers fill only a few scattered
seats in the desolate rows. I climb the stairs to the ladies' gallery and
from there peek down on the men's section to look for Len. It is easy
to find him: He stands out like a sore thumb among the dozen or so
shabbily dressed, elderly, dispirited men.

The ladies' gallery is empty: I am the only woman worshipper.

The voice of the cantor is lost in the vacuum. It reverberates timidly, an incongruous little voice in the vast empty space.

After the services, I head toward the front lobby of the synagogue
where I am to meet Len. As I descend the stairs from the ladies' section, a tall man, his frightened face topped by a black beret, climbs
the stairs to meet me. He addresses me on the landing, in whispered
Hungarian: "Madam," he mutters, looking around furtively, "may I
speak to you? May I ask you some questions?"

I am startled. "Why, of course. But . . . what questions?"

"Madam, I have a daughter. She's married to a foreigner. Her
husband has just finished his medical studies in Italy, and they
want to . . ." Suddenly he stops, and his face breaks into a wide

grin. Assuming a familiar tone, he says aloud: "What a lovely jacket, madam. But isn't it too warm? Let me help you take it off." He reaches for the back of my collar, saying once again, "Let me help you."

I am taken aback. I step backward to move out of his reach, saying, "No. It's not warm. No, thank you, I don't want to take it off."

Who is this madman? What does he want? As I walk quickly down the stairs to escape him, leaving him on the landing, the man's frightened, pleading voice follows me: "Forgive me, madam. Forgive me, please. Please don't go! Forgive me. I didn't mean to frighten you." His voice barely a whisper, he goes on: "Do you see that man with the black attaché case? He's an informer. He passed us deliberately just now, eavesdropping . . . As I was saying: My son-in-law is a physician, and he wants to live in Israel . . ."

Once again, he stifles his voice. I look up and see that the little man with the black attaché case is approaching; he says something in Slovak to the man in the black beret.

As I walk on, the man in the beret calls after me: "I hear there's a reception downstairs. Are you coming?"

"Yes," the little man answers in my place. "I'm going."

"Madam, are you coming?" the man with the beret repeats.

"I . . . I don't know. I'm waiting for my husband."

When we reach the main lobby I see Len coming out of the men's section.

The tall man with the beret and the little man with the attaché case walk together toward the room where the reception is to take place. Len had also been informed about the reception, which is being hosted by the new president of the congregation. "I think we should attend," Len says. "It could turn out to be an interesting experience. It would give us a chance to observe an aspect of Jewish life in this baffling city."

I agree, so we enter the small room, already filled to capacity. About fifteen men sit around one table, and about six or seven women at another. Wine and cake are served, and the men sing traditional Jewish songs.

The tall man in the beret and the little man with the attaché case sit next to each other. I attempt to make eye contact with the man in the beret; perhaps he was looking for an opportunity to speak to me again, to ask his questions. But his eyes keep avoiding mine. His face is impassive. He acts as if he has never seen me before. The two men chat amicably with each other, and then join in the singing.

Did the scene on the stairs actually happen? As time goes on, I become more and more convinced that the entire episode must have been a figment of my imagination.

The men stop singing, and the president of the congregation is asked to speak. He delivers a brief prepared lecture on the weekly portion of the Torah, and everyone gives it their rapt attention, including the man in the black beret and the man with the black attaché case. There is nothing but peace and camaraderie in this room. Anything but solidarity and the study of the Torah is inconceivable. My perception of furtive questions and informers is absurd. What is happening to me?

On our way to Mrs. Katz's for the midday meal, Len shares his impressions. He felt the services were strictly traditional, and this surprised him. One of the congregants befriended him, and gave him a rundown on people in the community. They all desecrated the Sabbath, he said, and ate non-kosher food. Yet, strangely, they stuck to the traditional form of worship, observing even the minutiae of traditional conduct in the synagogue.

"There was a man in the synagogue who attempted to ask me some questions in Hungarian," Len remarks. "I told him I did not speak Hungarian, but that you did. He was very keen on talking to you. Did he approach you after the services?"

"Was he wearing a black beret?"

"Yes, I believe he was."

"Thank God!"

"What's the matter? Why is that so important?"

"Now I know I'm not going insane. I almost believed I was."

"Why? What happened?"

I tell Len the strange tale, and we both wonder what the man wanted. "All I know is that it had to do with Israel—about his son-in-law and daughter wanting to get to Israel," I speculate.

"But what about the little man with the attaché case? Is he indeed an informer?" Len asks.

"The whole story is highly suspect. Perhaps the man in the black beret is suffering from delusions."

"Perhaps we could ask Viola. Would Viola know if there are informers, even in the synagogue?" Len suggests.

"Would she admit it? And would she take kindly to such questions?" I wonder aloud.

We were going to visit Viola and Samira on our way to Nesporova. We decided to broach the subject during our visit.

The two women receive us like long-lost relatives. We have much to talk about—our move to the Carlton, dinner at Mrs. Katz's, our impressions of the city and the synagogue. When I bring up the strange episode on the synagogue steps, Viola is surprised by my attitude.

"What's so strange about it?" she asks defensively. "Of course the little man with the black attaché case was an informer. What's wrong with that? There are informers everywhere. I'm sure there are many of them among the staff at the Carlton Hotel. The man in the black beret was wise not to speak to you in front of an informer—especially with the kind of questions he had about Israel. The authorities do not look kindly on people who have family in Israel. Or who intend to move there."

When she sees my indignation Viola adds: "Informers are part of the system. They are necessary. Every system has them. One learns to live with them, tolerate them. They are performing a function, sometimes a vital function. Vital functions are often unpleasant."

I am aghast at Viola's matter-of-fact justification of informers. Viola, the idealist!

"Do you consider informing morally acceptable? How about individual freedom? Do you consider the curtailment of individual freedom moral?"

Viola does not quite understand what I mean by *individual freedom*. The concept is foreign to Viola, the classic Communist. Her priorities are totally different. The individual does not matter in Communist society. As upset as I am, I know I am treading on thin ice and must mask my outrage at the distorted sense of morality that emerges from Viola's argument.

One does not argue with believers—especially if one is a guest in their Paradise.

On our way to Mrs. Katz's, I translate my discussion with Viola to Len, and when he hears it, he is just as disturbed as I am by Viola's attitude about informers. We both wonder about the man in the black beret who made an attempt to beat the system, and who, as a penalty, must live in constant fear. What a shame that I was not able to help him!

CHAPTER TWENTY-FIVE

Bratislava Nightlife

MRS. KATZ'S NOONTIME SABBATH MEAL IS A STUDY IN INGENUITY. LACKING meat, she has prepared *cholent*, the traditional meat-bean-and-potatoes Sabbath dish, with bits of salami. This is followed by reconstituted chicken: chicken parts that had been boiled in last night's soup, now doused with some garlicky liquid. And then last night's squash, now chilled. For dessert, the perennial gooseberries, and tea.

It is obvious that her menu required a great deal of thought. With no fruit but gooseberries, with no vegetables but an occasional green pepper or squash, with no meat but salami, the Czechoslovak house-wife's culinary skills are tried to the utmost. The kosher kitchen is an even greater challenge.

After lunch, Len and I decide to visit the famous Pressburg Cas-tle. We head for the Palisades, and from there the climb begins. The climb up the steep hill is interminable in the brilliant sunshine, and by the time we reach the Castle courtyard, we welcome the rich shade of the towering elms.

Unfortunately, the Castle is closed. "Let's tour the grounds instead!" I suggest, and Len seconds the motion. The courtyard is an exquisite enclosure with well-tended lawns and pebbled paths and a spectacular view of the city. A bench perched on a protruding rock as if suspended in midair above the Danube offers an ideal observa-tion post. The Castle itself is an unusual structure—a perfect square building with a flat roof and four towers, one on each angle of the square. To my surprise, the towers now have pointed rooftops. In my childhood, they, too, were flat on top, making the castle look like an inverted table with its four legs in the air. It was a most extraordinary sight, probably the most intriguing castle in the world.

Legend had it that throughout its long and stormy history, the Castle mysteriously burned down several times. In the late 1700s the roof and the tops of the towers were burned down for the last time. Since that time, until 1951, it was a beautiful, romantic ruin, haunted by its elusive past. But in 1951, the Czechoslovak government restored it, and now it is an ordinary structure, a municipal office building like so many others.

The sun moves behind the bridge and lights up the Danube in a festival of crimson. In the reddish-purple glow the city lies prostrate and vulnerable at our feet. In the foreground the blue tower of the Coronation Church rises above the rest. At the tip of its lanky Gothic spire, instead of a cross, a bejeweled crown glistens. A thought makes me spring to my feet:

"Len, wouldn't you like to see the Church of Coronation? Do you see that spectacular blue spire in the foreground, with the brilliant crown on top? If we walk fast downhill, we can get there before dark."

"Why not? Let's go!"

The spire is our guide. We hurry downhill through the Palisades, along winding, medieval cobblestone alleys, narrow and treacherously curving. Sometimes we lose sight of the blue spire, and do not know which way to turn. But then it bobs up again among the countless other spires and cupolas. We follow the spire through dank courtyards and crumbling ruins. We pick our way through musky passages. The setting sun is our challenge. We have to get there before dark, so that Len should be able to see the intricate carvings on the oak portals, the bas-reliefs, the exquisite architecture.

We have to get there before the doors close. It is a daunting chase, but finally, after a tentative turn into a dubious unpaved alley, the blue structure of the Coronation Church towers right before us!

The sun had sunk behind the bridge and the exterior is plunged in half shadows. Heavy iron gates block the entrance. A huge, rusty lock dangles on the gates and a small note in three languages—Slovak, German, and Hungarian—is pasted above: HOURS DAILY 9–1 2 AND 1–5; SATURDAY 9–1 2; CLOSED SUNDAY.

"Never mind," says Len. "We'll come back some other time."

"There's no other time. Tomorrow it's closed. On Monday is the exhumation. On Tuesday we are scheduled to take the caskets to Vienna. On Wednesday, we are scheduled to leave for home, if all goes according to plan."

If . . . An involuntary shudder reverberates through my body.

Darkness falls. The lights of the city appear one by one, and the Danube, this old, wise, silent river, mirrors both the darkness and the lights. The masts of the ships moored at the bank grow taller in the shadows, and the new bridge dotted by lights juts unexpectedly into the faintly luminous sky.

As we begin our walk across the bridge, a cool mist starts to swirl in the breeze above the river. It laps at my bare legs like an icy spray.

"Your hands are like ice," Len cries. "Let's go back to the hotel, get our raincoats, and return for a cup of coffee in the café on top of the bridge."

I am reluctant to give up my idea of a walk across the bridge now. Ever since we crossed it en route from Vienna, I had been anticipating a reunion with my beloved river from atop the bridge. It would be dark by the time we return, and I would not see the river as I had hoped, from high above.

I was not familiar with this part of the Danube, this wide waterway near Bratislava spanned by giant bridges and sailed by enormous ships. My Danube was a small branch near Samorin hugged by green shrubbery, its banks sloping along wide-open meadowland. Yet it is the same river. I know its pulse in my heart. I sense its rhythm deep within. I'm still prone to its magnetic pull, its irresistible attraction.

"Come, darling," Len urges. "You'll catch your death of cold here. Let's hurry back to the hotel. We'll call Viola and Samira and invite them to join us for a cup of coffee at the café. They'd probably like that."

Viola and Samira are thrilled with the invitation.

"How splendid!" Viola exclaims. "We'll meet you at the Carlton in half an hour."

Before leaving the hotel, Samira suggests that we check the café's closing time, as most places in Bratislava close at nine. It was already eight-thirty. Samira's hunch turns out to be right: The café is closed.

"What does one do in Bratislava on a Saturday night after nine?" I ask Samira.

"Not much," the two women say in unison.

"Perhaps some Hungarian wine cellars will be open," Samira suggests.

"Hungarian wine cellars? Gypsy music!" Len's face brightens.

"No gypsy music," Viola hastens to inform him. "Just wine cellars. If we are lucky."

We are not lucky. The first "quaint little spot" that Samira suggests is closed, the door bolted.

We walk for almost an hour before we reach the next "quaint little wine cellar" in the basement of a dilapidated house. We have to pick our way through rubble in order to reach the entrance, which is boarded up. There is no sign to indicate whether it would ever reopen.

Finally I propose that we find an open wine cellar, even if it was not so "quaint." Lo and behold, the next wine cellar we reach is open! It is bare and poorly lit. The heavy aroma of stale wine permeates the air. By now we are hungry, thirsty, and tired, so we sit at a corner table and Samira places our orders. Two glasses of wine for herself and Viola, two mugs of beer, for Len and myself. Hearing the word "beer," the waiter shakes his head: "No beer. We serve only wine."

Len and I cannot drink wine that is not produced under proper supervision. Tired, thirsty, and dispirited, we scramble to our feet.

The next wine cellar also does not serve beer. Neither does the third. In the third wine cellar the waiter breaks the conspiracy of silence. He confides in us that beer is too cheap; the turnover is too low for profit.

It is true. Czech beer, the best in the world, costs about 10 cents for a large glass. The same glass of beer costs 85 cents in Budapest, $3 in Vienna. In Czechoslovakia beer is subsidized by the government in order to make it available for average workers because it is an integral part of their diet. Len and I would have been glad to pay more, but you do not have the liberty to pay more. The price is controlled. That's the irony: Because one could not buy it for more, one could not buy it at all!

"Let's go to the Carlton; perhaps the café there is still open!" I propose, and the others join me in my resignation to have coffee in place of beer or wine.

The café is closed, but in the basement we discover an attractive pub, which, miracle of miracles, serves both wine and beer!

The evening ends on a happy note.

CHAPTER TWENTY-SIX

Rabbi Moshe Sofer

ON OUR LAST NIGHT BEFORE PARTING FOR THE EXHUMATION VIOLA PROMISED to make arrangements for a visit to the tomb of Rabbi Moshe Sofer, the eighteenth-century Talmudic scholar known the world over as "Hatam Sofer."

"We will join you on this expedition," Viola declared, and I could not believe my ears. Weren't Jewish roots antithetical to Communist ideology?

I am doubly glad for her decision to join us, and now we are waiting for mother and daughter to join us for the tram ride to the famous site.

Soon Viola and Samira arrive at the train stop, and all of us board the next canary-yellow streetcar heading north. The train winds its way alongside the riverbank. On our left, the river shimmers like a bejeweled snake, and on our right, the hills are covered with deep green forest, calm and expectant, still partially plunged in shadows.

The tram makes a sudden turn and comes to a screeching halt.

Viola indicates that we have arrived. We file out of the car and follow Viola to a small traffic diamond in the midst of onrushing traffic. Cars, buses, trucks, and motorcycles zigzag like lightning all about us and rush at breakneck speed into the gaping mouth of a tunnel carved out of sheer rock immediately ahead.

What on earth are we doing in the midst of all this traffic, waiting in the middle of this grassy traffic island?

"We're waiting for the custodian of the tomb," Viola says, as if reading my thoughts.

"But why here, in the middle of nowhere?"

"Ah, there she is!" Viola cries without answering my question.

Mrs. Hahn's scarf-wrapped head bobs up in the distance. She mumbles an apology for being late, produces a huge metal key ring from her bag, and goes down on her knees in the tall grass. What's going on here? Fumbling in the grass she locates an indentation, and, parting the thick growth with considerable effort, exposes a small trapdoor. There is a loud click; the lock springs open after the custodian inserts several keys into the large rusty hole. Even though the lock is open, however, the trapdoor does not yield to her efforts to lift it.

"Let me help you, madam," says Len, leaning forward and reaching for the trapdoor handle. Len's powerful tug at the mud-encrusted handle does the trick. The heavy metal door rises in a quivering wide arc and slams down heavily on the grassy ground, exposing, to our astonishment, a dark, gaping, square hole in the center of the emerald island!

Steep steps lead straight into the bowels of the earth.

We follow the custodian, groping blindly downward. Why are we descending into this underground tunnel underneath the Bratislava-Vienna highway?

The custodian mutters something about a light switch. She finds it, and all at once a pale, eerie illumination emanates from a naked bulb dangling from a long cord. We are in an underground burial chamber cluttered with a large number of topsy-turvy gravestones. A chest-high mound runs the length and width of the chamber allowing only a narrow passage all around. Half-burned candles and puddles of hardened wax fill the spaces between the toppling grave markers.

Like helpless ancient drunks on skid row, these strangely entrapped tombs spell a sense of utter desolation and despair.

What is the meaning of all this? What are we doing here? Whose graves are these? Has Viola made a mistake?

All at once I notice a tall white monument propped against the wall, apart from the others. It looms ghostlike out of the shadows cast by the single lightbulb. With startling vividness the black lettering glitters against the gleaming white surface: RABBI MOSHE SOFER.

"The Hatam Sofer! Here, in this cellar?" I shout in shock. "My God, how did his tomb get here?"

"This is not his tomb—only the tombstone. His tomb is over there." The custodian points to a small marker on the mound among the others. "Rabbi Sofer is buried there. But his tombstone was too tall for the ceiling. It had to be placed here on the ground."

"I don't understand. What is his grave doing here, in this . . . this manhole under a speedway?"

Mrs. Hahn looks baffled. "I'm not sure. You see—"

"I remember now," Viola interjects. "I remember the issue, the background to the story. This is where the old Jewish cemetery used to be. The Pressburg cemetery is one of the oldest Jewish graveyards in Europe. The site of the whole construction up there—the highway, the tunnel, the ramps onto the new bridge—all of that used to be part of the Jewish graveyard. But the graveyard was in the way of the highway project, so it had to be liquidated. The city council notified the Jews that they had to disinter their dead and move them elsewhere, higher up, a few kilometers up the mountain."

"When did this happen?"

"I believe at the beginning of the German occupation. It was part of the German plan to connect all parts of the Reich with superhighways. Somehow, through clandestine contacts, a substantial sum of

Jewish money passed into the right hands, and a number of ancient graves, Hatam Sofer and his disciples, were left undisturbed. When the ground was raised for highway construction, a small enclosure around the graves was left hollow, creating this underground burial chamber."

"It must have taken a lot of Jewish money."

"American Jewish organizations, mostly; U.S. dollars did the trick."

"How do you know all this? Weren't you in Palestine then?"

"Yes, I was. But I heard details from close associates. Some of them were involved. It was a complex business."

Len is busy with the jammed flash in his camera. Finally, he resigns himself to taking shots with the aid of the lightbulb.

The sudden impact of brightness comes as a shock when we emerge from the subterranean cemetery. I am thinking of the sunny Jerusalem hilltop, which awaits the remains of my grandparents. Will the remains of Hatam Sofer and his disciples be forever imprisoned in this dank manhole in the belly of Bratislava? Are they condemned to eternal exile in a foreign land?

The heavy metal trapdoor slams shut. The thick greenery obliterates once again the entrance to the obscure burial chamber, which holds a precious sliver of Jewish history, a fragment of the collective Jewish body shattered so ruthlessly by this latest violent convulsion of the Diaspora.

CHAPTER TWENTY-SEVEN

A Rude Reminder

"IT'S FIVE O'CLOCK. YOU ASKED TO BE AWAKENED."

I remember, and my heart skips a beat. "Thank you," I say to the hotel telephone operator, and hop out of bed.

Today is the big day. The taxi will be here in an hour. By seven, we have to be in Samorin. I awaken Len. All of our documents—a wad of permits, receipts, and contracts—have to be packed. White sheets, sandwiches, passports. Even a small can of black paint . . .

Every muscle in my body is tense. What if the taxi does not show? What if the gravediggers forget the date? What if the tin containers aren't ready? What if the customs officer has other appointments? What if Comrade Radek has changed his mind? What if . . . what if?

"What are these for?" Len is referring to the raincoats I'm holding. "It's nice out today. Look at the sunshine," he says triumphantly as he points out a faint yellow streak on the carpet.

"Just in case," I whisper sheepishly. "There's no shelter at the cemetery."

Len shrugs and flings the raincoats over his shoulder.

At 6:00 a.m. the taxi does not show. I run to the square and approach one of the taxis that idles nearby. The driver has to check with "Central." Central bids the driver to wait. We have no choice. We stand around on pins and needles, and wait. For what? The driver does not know.

Twenty minutes later, Central gives the driver permission to drive us to Samorin. The car moves at a snail's pace in the early-morning traffic. But by seven o'clock we manage to reach the out-skirts of Samorin, and several minutes later the taxi pulls up in front of the offices of the Burial Commission. Comrade Mihalna is deep in excited conversation with two men and a woman, and pays no attention to us. Neither the gravediggers nor the tinsmiths are to be seen.

Len and I listen to the sounds of the heated debate, and wonder what to do next. Half an hour later we still wait and wonder. Not a single worker in sight. Is this a slow realization of my worst fears?

The hysterical group finally leaves the room, and I approach my former classmate. In low tones she informs me that during the night a young boy had hanged himself and the body had been sent to Bratis-lava for an autopsy. This was the boy's family, grieving and indignant, the woman weeping and the men shouting menacingly. The autopsy had been ordered without their consent.

The door flings open and several solemn-faced men and women, all dressed in black, file into the office. Irena whispers in panic: "Jesus Maria, they're here already! The funeral . . . I'm not ready. Their daughter drowned on Saturday." In her panic Irena gives no indication that she is aware of the exhumation also scheduled for this morning.

At eight o'clock Comrade Radek arrives, perspiring profusely and just as profusely apologetic for his lateness. People come and go, and the exhumation seems to have been forgotten. Finally we dis-cover the problem: The hearse took the suicide victim to Bratislava, and there is no transportation for us to the cemetery! The gravedig-gers have made their own way, and the tinsmiths have ample time to deliver the containers later.

"How about a taxi?" I ask Irena.

"The taxi is occupied elsewhere," she says with finality, and I understand that Samorin must have only the one taxi. As luck would have it, at nine a friend of Irena passes by in his car and she asks him to drive us to the cemetery. As we are about to leave, Irena calls me aside and suggests I pay the man twenty-five crowns for his efforts.

"The sum is somewhat generous," she apologizes. "But, under the circumstances . . ."

I am grateful, and sit next to the driver with rising spirits. Len and Comrade Radek get into the back and we take off for the cemetery. At the fork in the road I remind the driver to take the right lane.

"The right? You're mistaken, miss. The right takes you to the Jewish graveyard. The cemetery is to the left."

"It's the Jewish cemetery we want."

The man gives me a sharp glance. He drives on for a few minutes without speaking, then starts to talk about his wartime experiences on the Ukrainian front with the Hungarian armed forces. In the Ukraine he "saw Jews lined up and shot: men, women, children, babies . . ." He and his entire unit were engaged in the shootings.

"I had nothing against those Jews, but an order is an order," he declares matter-of-factly. "We were told to shoot, so we shot. It was an order like any other. I shot twenty, maybe twenty-five Jews. There were hundreds of them. Maybe a thousand. Jews complain that six million were killed. That's a lie. It couldn't have been six million. No way. I was there. I saw it all. It was maybe a million or two, not more."

I look at his face—unremarkable features, fleshy jaw, square forehead, blank eyes focusing on the road. Is this the face of a mass murderer? I look at the man's hands. Those hands killed Jewish children. Now they hold the wheel of the station wagon. The very hands, the same fingers had cocked a trigger, and little Jewish children shrieked, mothers with infants in their arms fell to the ground . . . Jewish blood spurted into the sky.

"I had nothing against those Jews. It was an order like any other," he repeats. "And the Jews, they are bent on revenge against the whole world; they want the whole world destroyed, that's what they want. They incite America to start World War Three. They know World War Three would destroy the whole world. And for what? Because we followed orders? I was a good soldier, a good Hungarian. Jews always wanted trouble. Now they start up with the Arabs, and with Russia. The Arabs want peace and the Soviet Union wants peace. They're peace-loving nations. America and Israel are warmongers. They won't stop until they plunge the world into war. Jews have always wanted trouble; that's why they had to be killed. Mercilessly. Even their little bastards!" His voice rises and his face is turning red. "I would not ever hesitate to kill Jews again!"

The man is working himself into a frenzy. He drives unevenly, zigzagging from side to side. The station wagon keeps crashing against overgrown branches.

"I will kill Jews again!" he screams. "I'll shoot them on sight! How dare they cause war again? All Jews deserve to be shot on sight!"

Comrade Radek reaches up and squeezes my arm lightly. He leans over and whispers: "Don't say a word, please. Please."

I gulp. It is an effort to breathe. My temples throb, but I keep silent. With teeth clenched I grip the door handle as the car careens and crashes into the underbrush. The engine stalls, and the three of us hop out of the car. I thrust three ten-crown notes into his hand and flee into the jungle that is the Jewish graveyard.

The man's voice rings out: "What's this—thirty crowns? That's all you give me? Do you know the price of transporting Jews to the graveyard? Do you?"

The three of us walk on silently into the jungle.

"Thank you for not saying anything," Comrade Radek says. I look at him and see his blue eyes are brimming with tears. "And thank you for allowing me to join you."

I'm in shock. Is this possible? Can it be that Comrade Radek, the Communist functionary, the stolid Slovak bureaucrat, is a Jew?

CHAPTER TWENTY-EIGHT

Cosmic Drama in the Jungle

THE GRAVEDIGGERS, SHORT AND STURDY LIKE TREE TRUNKS, STAND AT THE second clearing, with shovels, axes, and sledgehammers piled on their shoulders. I spot a strip of pink toilet paper fluttering in the distance against the deep green foliage. On Thursday I had tied that strip to a tree branch to mark the path to the gravesite, not really expecting to find it here three days later. But there it is, a fluttering pink marker, announcing that we had arrived at the right spot in the deep green wilderness.

Stooping low under the heavy bough, I crawl into the grove. Len heaves the bough far above the ground and holds it with both hands high enough for the others to pass into the grove. The gravediggers, as soon as they find themselves in the interior of the copse, begin to clear the undergrowth in the direction of the graves. Reaching the graves, they swing their sledgehammers high in the air, and, bringing them down with brutal force, deal heavy blows to the concrete covering on the first grave.

The sun is high and an oppressive heat hangs above the cemetery. Discarding the enormous blocks of broken concrete, the gravediggers start digging. With each shovel full of dry clumps of earth that they send flying into the air, the gravediggers' heads seem to sink lower and lower into the ground. It is my grandfather's remains that they are nearing underneath the layers of resistant soil.

Soon only the tops of the gravediggers' heads are visible amid flying clumps of dirt.

"Jancsi!" I call to the elder of the two. "How will you know when you're near the bones?"

"We'll know. The sounds get hollow, even before we reach the coffin."

I wonder if there is going to be a coffin at all. In some areas, Jewish custom dictates that graves be lined only with wooden planks. In other places the body is conveyed directly "unto the dust" in compliance with the biblical verse.

"As soon as you think you're approaching the bones, you and Sandor must climb out of the pit. We will do the rest, my husband and I. Do you understand? It's very important that you remember this. The very minute you feel you're near the body, you must call me."

"That's all right, ma'am. I'll remember."

The hole is almost two meters deep now. The gravediggers' heads have long since disappeared. The three of us keep a silent vigil in the shade of the underbrush. Huge swarms of shimmering insects buzz about our heads, in angry protest over the invasion of their domain. Now pieces of rock and reddish-brown clumps of earth fly from the pit, a rhythmic tribal dance of death. The heap at the edge of the pit is growing higher and higher.

"No sign of bones yet, Jancsi?"

"No, ma'am."

"How deep is the hole now?"

"About two meters."

"Two meters! And no sign of bones? How deep is a grave? Normally, I mean."

"Not this deep. Less than two meters."

The clumps of earth are dark brown now, and they scatter in small particles. I bend down and address the bald spot on top of Jancsi's head.

"Any bones yet, Jancsi? How much deeper?"

"Only God knows. This is deeper than I've ever been."

"Jancsi, do you think something is wrong?"

"Maybe the body shifted. In so many years the body could've shifted." Jancsi scratches his head. "Or, maybe there's nothing left. Bones crumble, you know. Bones crumble and become like particles of earth. Maybe nothing but earth is left in this grave."

"You mean to say that . . . that what you're digging right now could be bone particles . . . that have turned into earth particles? Is it possible you wouldn't know the difference? Jancsi, is that possible?"

"Everything's possible." He spits out the words between toothless gums. His words like disembodied sounds rise ominously from the depth of the grave. "Everything's possible."

The sun stands high in the sky. Searing heat floods the grove. I shiver. We may be digging an empty grave. We may be flinging the disintegrated particles of my grandfather's body out of the grave, scattering them like so many grains of dust. What should I do? Should I halt the digging?

"Ma'am," Jancsi says, turning his brown, dirt-encrusted face upward, his eyes glinting against the glare, "I'm striking wood." He bends down, picks up a piece of reddish-brown matter, and hands it up to me. I kneel at the edge and reach down until I can grasp the spongy, moist thing. A heavy odor of decay rises to my nostrils.

"What does this mean?"

"This must be the coffin. The bones are directly underneath. Do you want us to stop digging?"

"Of course!" I shriek. "Of course. Come right up!"

A light quivering takes hold of my body. I stare into the grave and see the dark, decaying wooden planks encrusted in the earth. I am looking into the depth that separates the living from the dead. I gaze trembling into the open grave and the oracle of the Prophet Ezekiel resonates like an orchestra within me:

> *Behold, I open your graves, and will raise you from your graves, my people, and I will bring you to the Land of Israel . . .*
> *And you shall know that I am the Lord by opening your graves and raising you from your graves . . .*
> *And the bones . . . are very many . . . very dry . . .*
> *And I shall put my spirit into you, and you shall live, and I shall put you onto your Land . . .*

What lies there, underneath these dark, musty pieces of wood? Is it an intact skeleton? Or only parts of a skeleton, the other parts having decayed and disintegrated long ago? What color are the bones— white and ghostly, like those found in scary tales? Will they contrast shockingly with the dark earth?

I did not know my grandparents. They both died before I was born. I did not know them, yet I have always known them. They have always been there, in my childhood, in my adolescent years. Their portraits hung in the bedroom. My grandmother's proud gaze and my grandfather's gentle, smiling eyes were part of my inner world. They formed the background against which I grew into adulthood. Memories of my grandfather's teachings provided guidelines for my own growth.

I call to Len, and he nimbly leaps into the grave. Prying the wooden planks one by one, he hands them to me until the entire length of the grave pit is clear of wood. No skeleton. With his fingers, Len probes the ground that is encrusted with gnarled tree roots and bits of debris.

"Nothing but decayed debris, fossilized bits of matter."

I hold my breath. "Are you sure?"

Len crouches on the bottom of the grave and digs his fingers deep into the crusty bronze morass. His brow is dripping sweat. The ground sways under my feet. *I shall raise you from your graves . . . And the bones . . . are very many . . .*

Where are my grandfather's bones?

Len is reaching up and in his hand there's an eerie whitish, rounded object. "Look!"

I gasp. "My God! The skull!"

"No. This is not the skull. It's porcelain. Half of a water jug. Look! Here's the other half!"

Len's outstretched arm delivers the two halves of an earthenware jug. I crouch, and slowly, with a tremor in my fingers, grip the strange objects, placing them next to each other in the grass. How strange. A perfect porcelain jug with a delicately shaped handle and spout! What is this jug doing here in the grave? And where are the bones? Is this a grave at all?

"Any sign of bones?"

Len continues probing the unresponsive layer of clay where the jug has left a round dent. The clump his fingers are palpating gives way bit by bit, and slowly he manages to pry it loose from the stubborn soil. He raises it high into the blinding glare of the sun. It's a cylindrical thing, reddish-brown like the earthen particles that cling to it. Long wooded projections like hardened plant roots hang about it on all sides, and two small square pieces of pottery stuck to one side make it look like a football with mock spectacles.

"This is the skull," Len says simply.

The skull! My grandfather's skull. I stand, paralyzed. Time, like a fossil, silent, is waiting.

"Take it, darling. Take it. This is your grandfather's skull."

My body goes numb. Like a mechanical robot, I reach without feeling. My trembling fingers have lost their sense of touch. I hold my grandfather's skull and place it slowly, mechanically, on the white sheet spread in the metal container the tinsmiths have just delivered. I reach again and again as Len hands me bronze-colored sticks of all sizes, one by one, after his fingernails pry them loose from the hardened clay. They look like petrified wood, dark, spongy, amorphous. But, they are bones: Len the physician names each one as he hands them to me:

"A vertebra. Here's another one. And another. Please count them. Remember, we have to have an exact count. Every bone must be accounted for." He scoops up a handful of brown circular bits. "Count all the vertebrae, darling, will you. The entire skeleton must be re-interred intact.

"This is a rib. Here's another. Here . . . a collarbone. These are pelvic bones. A kneecap; here, take it. Let me find the other one. Have you counted the ribs?"

I crouch at the edge of the pit. My mind is shut to the mechanics of what is happening. My hands move involuntarily, my fingers holding each bone without the sensation of touch. I place each bone automatically into the bedsheet-lined container. I notice that my hands have stopped trembling. My dread has long since dissipated into a mental fog. I work rhythmically with Len, and all is being accomplished methodically. We are cataloging and storing the skeleton, bone by bone.

I start to distinguish the bones. I count tibiae, femurs, shoulder blades . . .

The sun filters through the foliage with its scorching fury, and the grove turns into a heat trap. Mosquitoes, a buzzing cloud, keep circling above my head. I reach for a bone with one hand and with another fan off the mosquitoes. More vertebrae. Another rib . . . another leg bone . . . The mosquito cloud keeps growing. The sternum . . . jawbones. The heat and mosquitoes blend into an overwhelming humming presence about my head. I am a participant in the cosmic drama of life and death, yet I feel numb, empty. My mind is fixed on the task at hand. No other thought must penetrate my awareness.

Comrade Radek positions himself near the pit and helps with the count.

"It's finished," Len announces, with sweat pouring down his temples. "It's finished. There are no more bones in the grave. I've searched the dust carefully."

He grips the edge of the pit with powerful fingers and swings his body to the surface. His face is covered with red mud. Perspiration has plastered his hair to his forehead. Mud and sweat stain his navy blue T-shirt and his elbows are bleeding. "It is done," he whispers with finality.

"Len, we've recovered none of the small bones, like fingers, toes. We have none of those."

"True. I've found no small bones. Either they are so deeply embedded in the earth that it's impossible to find them, or they have disintegrated."

"I have a strange compulsion about this thing, Len. I must see for myself. I apologize . . . I would like to go down and see for myself. I must check it out. I know it's an insane compulsion. Forgive me, but would you help me down there?"

"By all means."

The two men lower me into the narrow pit. God! It is a purgatory down here! The vertical rays of the sun have turned the clay walls and bottom of the pit into an oven. Swarms of mosquitoes add to the burning sensation. I marvel at Len's stoic endurance, spending two hours down here without a word of complaint. I will not be able to bear it longer than a few minutes.

I carefully sift the surface clay with my fingers, reaching into every corner. I work my way from head to foot, palpating every particle of dust. There's nothing but clumps of clay. Mosquitoes swoop down on my arms and neck. They hiss as they penetrate the bare skin, and even my back through the fabric of my navy blue top. I work feverishly. I reach under the planks that line the sides of the grave.

A tiny tough clod has chanced its way between my fingers. I rub at it. Rub it again. The mosquitoes sting my back with renewed fury. The clay crumbles and reveals a minuscule smooth object, a small pebble. I strike it against a rock protruding from the wall of the grave. It does not resound. It cannot be a pebble. Yet it is not a piece of wood; it has a different texture. What is it?

"Len, look—look at this. What do you think it is?"

Len takes the tiny thing and examines it. "It's a pebble."

"Strike it against a rock, Len. Does it sound like a pebble?"

Len strikes it against a chunk of cement. "It's a bone. A small finger bone—a metatarsal. Amazing. I thought these small bones disintegrated after a few years in the ground. Where did you find it?"

"Under the rotted planks in the side. I scraped it from the crack underneath the wood."

The wooden planks lining the sides of the pit slant inward. The grave has gradually been caving in on itself, and the sides meet the bottom of the grave at an acute angle. I reach again into the crack at the apex of the angle under the bottom plank where I found the bone, and start to scrape the earth with renewed vigor.

The mosquitoes attack with increased ferocity. I rip the kerchief off my head, and with it I whip the swarm to keep them at bay. With my left hand, I keep whipping above my head and with my right I scrape underneath the putrefied wood. A handful of dark brown clay yields a handful of bits, and they all turn out to be bones. Len examines them and finds that they constitute the entire right hand. Now I move to the left side of the pit and repeat the operation. Here I discover all the bones of the left hand. I search under the planks where I assume the feet must have been. My hunch proves right. They are all there, the entire set of bones that make up each foot.

I work like a demon, oblivious to the heat and the mosquitoes. All my fervor focuses on the stubborn, unyielding crust of the earth. Finally, my fingers pry from the rocklike clay bed a multitude of tiny bones. Len the clinician and Comrade Radek the bureaucrat exclaim in awe at the state of their preservation. Fifty-five years!

I continue to work with animal ferocity. My fingers scrape under the planks where the skull had been. There is no stopping now. My nails crack. Drops of sweat mingle with the desiccated earth. Finally my fingers, bruised and bleeding, close in on a handful of perfect, tiny isosceles triangles.

"Len! My God! What do you think these are?"

"Teeth! A complete set of teeth, in perfect shape. Incredible!"

"Look at them, Len! Beautiful, healthy teeth . . ." I quickly count the handful of teeth. "All thirty-two of them. Can you believe it?"

You inherited his smile, his warm, quick, ready smile . . . I hear Mother's voice. *You inherited his love of people, of children* . . . I hear Mother's voice, but I don't want to think about it. I shut my ears to Mom's voice. Please Mom, I don't want to remember. I can't; not now. It's a job, and I must accomplish it. I want to accomplish it for you, Mom.

I stretch on tiptoes and gently place the handful of teeth into my husband's cupped palm.

Crouching in the ovenlike pit, I scrape the scorching surface again and again. Little insects burrow deeper into the clay. I must not think. I must recover every particle while the moment lasts. I must not let the moment slip between my fingers. It's up to me to bring every bone of my mother's father from exile to Jerusalem, to the Land of Israel.

"I've counted all the small bones. They're all here. You won't find any more in the grave. Why don't you stop now, and come up?" Len's voice is pleading.

I cannot stop. Not yet. I have to see for myself, again and again. Are there really no more bones? Am I really not leaving any behind, somewhere in the crevices, somewhere underneath the decaying wood? I must not. I must not.

"The customs official has arrived," Len calls into the pit. "He wants to speak to you."

Frantically, I run my fingers through the entire length and width of the grave. I reach under the side planks with deft fingers. The mosquitoes have bitten my back and neck raw, and now they are hissing menacingly in my ears. Suddenly, I am blinded by a sudden burst of cement dust. The gravediggers have finished clearing the undergrowth around my grandmother's grave and have started pounding the concrete slab covering it. A dense, white dust cloud rises from under their heavy blows.

Len's voice is muffled by the noise. "I cannot talk to him," he shouts. "You must come up. Please! You'll not find any more bones! Believe me. Please come up."

"Len—give me one more minute."

I panic. The finality of it . . . Have I really completed the job? The heat is unbearable. And the mosquitoes attack again and again. It is difficult to breathe; the thick cement dust makes even thinking difficult.

Len's voice filters through the cement cloud: "Please. You must speak to the inspector."

I raise my head and speak into the white dust: "Will you help me?"

Len reaches down with both hands. I grasp his hands and fasten a foot above a piece of rock in the side. My head is reeling. I am unable to hoist myself onto the rock. The heat and the cement dust are suffocating.

"I can't make it, Len."

"Wait—I'll call the comrade to help."

The two men reach down and pull me out of the grave like a rag doll. I lie on the ground for a few seconds, feeling the earth tremble and heave with the rhythmic blows of the gravediggers' hammers. Are they cracking open the face of the earth?

Finally I get to my feet and see the concerned looks of the two men. "I'm okay," I say, smiling wanly, and I tie the kerchief about my hair. Lucky I did not leave it behind in the grave. "I'm fine now. Where's the inspector?"

I follow Len as he pushes his way through the thicket with determination. A young man in Russian-style military uniform stands in the clearing, his attention on the gravediggers' attempts to demolish the thick concrete slab. Despite their noise and dust, it looks like they've barely made a dent in it yet.

I introduce myself and the inspector nods courteously. "I understand you have one coffin ready," he states. "May I inspect it now?"

"The coffin is in there, beyond these bushes near the open pit. Wait here, please, and we'll bring it to you."

Just then I spot the tinsmiths, setting up their apparatus for soldering.

Len and Comrade Radek emerge from the grove, carrying the coffin. The white bedsheet wrapped around the bones glistens with stark brilliance in the midday sun.

"Oh, thank you," I call to the two men. "Please put it here." I point to a grassy knoll in the shade. Len and Comrade Radek reverently lower the coffin to the ground. Their faces are solemn and smudged with dirt; sweat is pouring down their necks.

I stoop low and slowly, reluctantly lift the sheet. The inspector's face stiffens, and he averts his gaze. He makes no attempt to examine the contents of the coffin. "Were there any gold teeth?" he asks in low tones.

"No. No gold teeth."

"This coffin—what metal is it?"

"Zinc."

"That's all," the inspector says, and walks away. "The coffin can be sealed."

Gently, I rewrap the sheet around the bones and crawl into the grove to find the lid of the casket. The inspector is making notations in his book.

Len fumbles in my handbag, draws out the Bible, and begins to recite the Psalms in a whisper. I find the piece of paper on which I have scribbled the lines of a poem, an apology I've composed in Hebrew, begging my Mom's dear father for forgiveness, for having disturbed his eternal rest. I choke with emotion as I attempt to read it. Sniffling and sobbing, I fold the wet paper and place it in the coffin.

The tinsmiths carry the coffin to their apparatus and begin to solder the lid to the metal container, sealing it all around.

"Do you have a wooden coffin?" the customs officer inquires. "The zinc casket has to be placed inside a wooden one. I have to place my seal on the outer coffin."

"It's right here."

I carry one of the two silver-painted wooden coffins from under the trees. But before the tinsmiths can place the wooden lid on the casket, I take my nail scissors from my handbag and scrape the Hebrew letters SIMHA ZVI on the black painted surface of the metal lid.

I will raise you from your graves and bring you to the Land of Israel . . .

The wooden lid is nailed down. The tinsmiths drill a small hole through the lid and the side of the coffin, run a wire through the holes, and then twist the ends of the wire into a loop. To this wire loop the customs officer affixes his seal. I draw a small can of glossy black paint out of my bag and, with a makeup brush, I paint the Hebrew name of my ancestor, SIMHA ZVI, on the outer casket.

The first coffin is ready for shipment.

CHAPTER TWENTY-NINE

Attack by "Evil Spirits"

ALL AT ONCE JANCSI'S SPADE STRIKES METAL! HE IS DIGGING MY GRAND-mother's grave, and the probing spade makes a curious discovery: The pit is lined with metal on all sides. What does this mean? Why a metal grave?

As Jancsi and Sandor dig deeper and deeper, the metal lining turns out to be a huge container, the size and shape of the grave itself. They dig and dig, and as they reach the bottom of the two-meter-deep container, they find it empty! There is no body in the metal container.

Jancsi and Sandor are ready to climb out of the pit. "We are through; we've done our job," Jancsi declares. "The grave we dug contains no body. Sorry, ma'am, but that's not our fault."

"But there must be a body in the grave!" My knees begin to quake. I must make them understand. My grandmother's body has to be here in this pit! This pit contains my mom's dear mother—I know it. I know it. Why can't they understand?

"The metal container must be removed from the pit," I say steadily. "Once removed, the grave will reveal the body. The metal container must be removed from the pit!"

"That's impossible," Sandor says. This is the first time I've heard him speak. "I've never seen anything like it. It makes no good sense to pull out the tin lining."

"We've done our job," Jancsi repeats resolutely. "We're coming up."

"Jancsi," I say as calmly as I can, while my knees are shaking, "it's true. You've done your job. You've dug the graves. But we don't have the second body. We cannot walk away from here without the second body. I'll pay you for your extra effort—just name your price. Let's get that container out of the pit."

The gravediggers stand motionless for a moment. Then Jancsi announces: "We're coming up." Sandor follows Jancsi's lead, and they climb out of the pit. When both reach level ground, the inspector turns to them and says, "You heard the American lady. Get a move on, men. I'll help you. Let's get on with it."

Now the gravediggers loosen the earth around the metal sheet with their spades, and everyone chips in. All grip the edge of the metal and start tugging at it. It takes almost ten minutes before the monstrous metal container is hoisted out of the pit. Underneath there is a layer of decaying wood.

"The body must be underneath the wooden planks," I say in a low, steady voice.

The gravediggers move to the rapidly vanishing shade of the underbrush. Len ignores them and climbs into the pit. One by one he pulls up the wooden planks and hands them to Comrade Radek until the very last plank is removed.

There, underneath, is a perfectly preserved skeleton, reposing on its side! I am mesmerized. I was not prepared for this. These are not "wooded" bones encrusted in the earth. This is a person, in an unmistakable attitude of calm repose. Are you Grandmother Leah, the proud beauty with the legendary strength of spirit? Is that you, Grandma, my mother's beloved mom, whose name she bestowed upon me with the hope that I would grow up to be like you, proud and strong and beautiful?

A cluster of flies buzzes about, and Len begins the work of exhumation. He hands me the bones in rapid succession and I place them swiftly into the bedsheet-lined casket. There is none of the agonizing guilt that accompanied the earlier exhumation. Here there is no violent wrenching of parts from their earthbound setting. This grave yields the bones willingly, and we respond with a sense of relief bordering on exhilaration.

In less than twenty minutes, the entire skeleton is transferred into the casket. Len reaches for the skull last. As he lifts the skull, he gives a bloodcurdling shriek. He clutches the side of his head and his face is distorted with pain.

"Len! What's happened?"

"In my ear! A sting—it's excruciating! Help . . . help me get out of here!"

Comrade Radek helps me pull Len out of the pit. A large bee is clinging to a red protrusion from his ear. Len winces as I remove the dead insect and pluck its stinger from the swelling. At that instant, a blanket of hissing bees descends upon us. A swarm swoops down on my face, and in seconds I am blinded by burning pain. Stings on my cheekbone close my left eye completely, and turn my right eye into a narrow slit. My lips become bulging protrusions, like the beak of a bird.

Above the unearthly hissing of the bee multitude, I hear Comrade Radek wailing loudly nearby. I kneel down and shake my head violently to dislodge the bees. Ripping the kerchief off my head, I slap at the bees on my face, shoulders, chest, and arms, slapping and waving until I am momentarily free.

Now I see Comrade Radek run wildly about, wailing, clutching his head in both hands. The customs officer is performing a strange St. Vitus dance, hopping up and down, waving his military cap, emitting loud, sharp shrieks. A thick blanket of bees covers the sky, turning daylight into night. Millions of bees, a dark hissing train, swoop back and forth among us, their targets. Millions of black shiny creatures with transparent wings swirl in sharp circles and charge with deadly swiftness and accuracy, again and again.

The tinsmiths are rolling in the tall undergrowth, the younger one groaning loudly, kicking in the air, the older one whimpering, his face buried in the grass. Comrade Radek is crouching now, his head between his knees, his blue beret pulled over his face. Len has disappeared between the trees. The gravediggers' legs dangle from under the foliage, their upper bodies invisible in the thicket. Now Len reappears from behind the trees, galloping and waving his hands, a deadly halo of bees circling his head.

The customs inspector is still doing his insane jig while waving his hat in the air, a cluster of bees perched on his bald patch. The bright red ribbon is gone from his hat; his jacket is open and his face is streaked with an intricate pattern of blood and dirt.

Several bees have crawled under my blouse. The searing pain from stings on my back and chest would have driven me wild had I had time to indulge in self-pity. But there is no time for such luxury. The swarm charges in formation again, and again. Several bees land again on my head and sting my scalp through the kerchief that I'd tied once again about my hair. The stings feel like electric drills penetrating my skull. I snatch the large towel I had brought from the hotel, slap the bees off my kerchief, and wrap the towel around my head and face. It's useless. With ferocious buzzing the entire hive seems intent on concentrating its assault against my head, and the savage stings penetrate even the thick towel.

I fling away the towel with part of the hive swarming in its folds, and shout like a madwoman: "Let's run! Let's run from here! Let's leave them behind!" I begin running through the clearing on the narrow, overgrown lane toward the cemetery exit. Like one possessed, I skip across the steep ditch and shoot through knee-deep grass. The customs inspector runs right behind me, huffing loudly, the metal buttons of his open jacket crashing against the brush. His hat is gone, and he is flailing with both hands in savage movements, widening his path in the green growth like a weak swimmer parting the waves at random. Len and Comrade Radek follow closely behind. The two tinsmiths bring up the rear. The gravediggers are nowhere to be seen.

The company races through the jungle with lightning speed. We gallop among trees with branches hanging so low that we have to crouch while running in order to pass under them.

Suddenly we emerge on the open road. The bees are gone. We look at each other, incredulous. The customs officer is unrecognizable. Large bumps cover his face and close his left eye. Comrade Radek has a hornlike protrusion on his forehead, and another on his scalp. Len has several small bumps on his face but complains most about one on his right shoulder. The skin on my arms, chest, and back is taut with swelling.

I manage to remove the stingers from my arms and offer to do the same for the others. The stingers are large, and it's easy to pluck them from the tightly swollen skin. I clear Len's shoulders, the inspector's bald patch and face, and Comrade Radek's bump above the eye. The tinsmiths treat each other, alternately plucking the bee stingers from each other's wounds.

We sit at the side of the road, stunned. We are dazed and traumatized by pain, bewilderment, panic, and a sense of helplessness. We are disheveled, smeared with blood and dirt, and badly shaken. No one breaks the shocked silence for some time.

"If I were superstitious . . ." Len begins, then falls silent.

"What if you were superstitious, Doctor?" The young inspector is eager to pursue the topic. "Doctor, what were you going to say?"

"If I were superstitious," Len continues, "I'd believe it was . . . well, it's as if some evil spirits wanted to prevent us from exhuming the remains. Those bees came out of nowhere. Where did they come from? They swooped out like phantoms, out of nowhere."

"They were no ordinary bees, that's for sure," one of the tinsmiths muses. "I've never seen anything like it. They were black! And huge!"

"They were wild bees," Comrade Radek says quietly. "Very unusual variety. Their sting is very large, too. And very painful. They are a rare sort."

"Like the sting of the devil," says the second tinsmith. "And they came like some spooky blitzkrieg—a bunch of killers from the skies."

"The suddenness of their appearance was extraordinary," Len adds. "And their attack, so swift and so fierce. Quite extraordinary."

The customs officer wishes to return to the subject of superstition. "I'm not superstitious, of course," he says, "but I thought the same thing. I thought: If I *were* superstitious, I'd be convinced that those were no real bees. They were evil spirits. Ghosts."

"But we are not superstitious," Len responds. He seems remarkably composed. The only one of us who is calm—bruised, covered with large red swellings, but unruffled, nonetheless. All the others are still in shock. The inspector is a pitiful sight, spitting on several handkerchiefs and applying the spit to his numerous swellings. The tinsmiths sit leaning against each other like two tin soldiers in a discarded toybox. Comrade Radek holds his head between his knees with his eyes closed, as if in a daze.

"We're not superstitious," Len repeats briskly. "So let's go back and finish the job."

"Go back? What are you saying? Are you serious?" I say. I cannot go back to the cemetery. I simply cannot face it.

"We must pull ourselves together and finish the job," Len urges. "We're almost done. Fifteen, twenty minutes more."

No one responds. No one moves.

"I can't," I say finally. "I can't, Len. Not now. Not today."

"It has to be today. We're almost done. We must finish today. We can't leave the graves open, the coffins unattended. How about all the workers, the supervisors—the hearse?"

"Not today, Len, please . . . I can't. Perhaps tomorrow."

"Darling," Len's voice is calm and firm. "Pull yourself together. It's okay. The bees are gone. Please tell the others—it's over, and we must get back. There's nothing to be afraid of. You must encourage the others. Tomorrow will be worse. If you don't go back now, right now, you won't do it later. Let's go, darling. Call the others."

The others respond to Len's cue. His demeanor and tone communicates nonverbally a message of strength and courage. The customs officer offers to drive into town and buy some insect spray to ward off the bees, should they return. The tinsmiths suggest building a fire, saying that the smoke would deter the bees. Comrade Radek does not say anything. He shakes his head, and when the company rises to begin the climb into the woods, he, too, follows.

My eyes fill with tears as Len helps me to my feet. "Thank you, Len," I whisper, and follow behind his slim neck and wide shoulders.

When we reach the gravesite, there's no sign of the bees. The gravediggers are sitting in the shade of a tree. They weathered the attack by hiding deep in the thicket. Bees avoid the shade, they explain, and as soon as the attack began, they crawled deep into it.

The skull is lying on its side in the empty grave. Did the bees emerge from under the skull? They burst into the air the moment Len had lifted the skull, making him their first casualty.

Now the grave is silent, and the solitary skull lies peacefully on its side. Len lowers himself into the grave and reaches for the skull. I hold my breath in terror.

"Look!" he calls out.

I'm shaking with fright as he holds up a pale pink object in his hand.

"Isn't it astounding? A set of dentures, in perfect condition. Just like new."

I stare. It's a set of false teeth, with several gold teeth in the upper row.

"It lay under the skull," says Len. "Apparently it slid out of the mouth as the body lay on its side."

How did it get there? Why was it buried with the body? Such a mundane thing: a set of teeth. And yet, at this moment it has assumed a supernatural dimension. Unlike organic matter, it has not decayed. It defied the laws of nature—death and time. For me, the dentures assume an existential reality, a bridge. I hold them in my hand, and through the object that had been in intimate contact with her, I become one with the mother who gave birth to mine.

The customs officer returns with the insect spray, and just then, a shadow covers the sun. Once again, the bees swoop out of nowhere, a black phantom force, once again poised for attack in precise formation. The customs officer sprays right and left, sending powerful streams of spray into the air. Bees start swarming around him in droves, following his every move. They are attracted by the chemical and hiss with joy as they alight on his shoulders, neck, hands, and even the spray can.

"Run into the shade!" I shout to him as Len draws me into the thicket. "Crawl under the brush!"

The tinsmiths have started a fire, and curls of smoke rise up to the sky. A light breeze fans the fire, spreading the smoke in all directions. The bees begin to disperse. They break ranks and begin to zigzag in confusion. Some shoot toward the sky and seem to be swallowed by the glaring sun. Others seem to disintegrate in the clouds of smoke. Within seconds, the bees vanish, just as suddenly and mysteriously as they had appeared.

All is silent again.

CHAPTER THIRTY

The Storm

THE POINT OF MY NAIL SCISSORS SCRAPES THE BLACK PAINT, AND AS I INSCRIBE the letters, I expose the original silver color of the tin. Soon, the name LEAH glistens brightly against the black background. Then, just like on my grandfather's coffin, I carefully paint the name on the lid of the outer coffin. The glossy black letters stand out against the bright silver surface.

Now Jancsi approaches, hat in hand: "We'd like to be paid now. My partner and I, we want to go home."

"Jancsi, don't you remember the graves must be filled? It's part of our deal. Also this pit here," I point at the open grave of Viola's father. "Will you?"

"We can't do it right now," he says. "We're tired. We'll come back after supper to finish the job."

Here we go again!

"Jancsi, I understand you're tired. You've worked hard. But the graves must be closed immediately, without any delay. It's an old tradition that graves should not be left open."

Jancsi repeats his promise to return after supper. He also repeats his demand to be paid immediately.

"Fine," I answer in despair. "But leave your shovels here. My husband and I will close the graves. All the graves must be closed."

The inspector intervenes once again: "Comrade, do as the lady says. Fill up the pits. Then you can go home."

Reluctantly, the gravediggers begin shoveling earth and chunks of cement into the three empty grave pits while the tinsmiths nail the second coffin shut and the inspector affixes his seal.

Suddenly, lightning slashes through the air and a deafening thunderclap quakes the jungle that has been plunged into darkness. Within seconds, heavy raindrops turn into vertical curtains of water veiling the green morass.

Comrade Radek and the inspector take off at a run, carrying one of the caskets. Len and the tinsmiths follow with the other. I bring up the rear of the galloping company, carrying our bags. As we run for our lives, brilliant flashes light up the wet wilderness. The track through the woods has turned into a rushing stream, and we emerge from the jungle soaked to the bone.

The grubby hearse near the cemetery entrance on the flooded open road seems to be floating on the surface of a raging river. Thunderclaps have become a steady drumbeat. The tinsmiths help the gravediggers heave the caskets into the hearse, then climb into their truck and take off after the hearse. The inspector urges us into his black limousine and quickly shuts the door against the translucent curtain of water that now splatters on the windows and the windshield, offering an impressionistic view of the jagged jungle.

The four of us huddle, shivering, in the spacious limousine while the inspector completes his paperwork. "I must write up my report," he informs us as he bends over a clipboard perched on his water-soaked knees. Water drips from the visor of his military cap onto the carefully penned document. I offer my towel to dry it. Comrade Radek is busy mopping his head and neck with a large handkerchief, carefully avoiding the sites of the bee stings that have turned into crimson swellings. Len and I are somewhat more comfortable under the cover of our raincoats.

The inspector ceremoniously hands me a copy of the completed document, simultaneously accelerating the car's engine.

"This calls for a drink!" Len exclaims, and the mood brightens instantly. Len always has his priorities straight. He is not thrown off course by the day's traumas, just as during the London blitz when he had "the perfect hand in poker" at the moment the building received a hit. The wall split right in front of him, and plaster tumbled from the ceiling, but Len refused to interrupt the game. It was "maddening" when his partners ran for shelter, ignoring Len's pleas to stay and finish the game!

The men happily accept Len's invitation for a drink at the Yellow Lark, the local tavern. Samorin looks as if it has just emerged from the Great Flood. The Yellow Lark is steaming with human vapor. It seems the inspector's uniform intimidated the throng of workers and farmhands crowding around large oaken tables. Eyes focus on our every move as the customs officer leads us to a vacant table.

I barely recognize myself in the washroom mirror. My face is smudged with dirt and badly ravaged by bee stings. My upper lip is still swollen, and a large bump on my left cheekbone gives my features a peculiar distortion.

I wash my face, comb my hair, and adjust the collar of my blouse. Dabs of facial cream from a small jar in my makeup kit revive my complexion, and with a touch of lipstick and mascara, I feel somewhat presentable.

The three men cluck their tongues and make surprised noises of approval when I join the table. I'm embarrassed for being secretly pleased with the response I evoked. How could I feel this way, today, of all days? The men joke a little and pay lavish compliments, and then the conversation reverts to the bees. The comrades complain bitterly; they have headaches, and their swellings are even redder than before. Len the physician suggests wet compresses and aspirin.

"And a mug of beer," he adds, smiling, and I translate. The comrades cheer and admit that the cool beer does indeed soothe their discomfort.

"Excellent beer," Len comments, "and I'm glad it worked."

The officer drains his second mug of beer before responding: "If the government discontinued the beer subsidy, there'd be a revolution."

Both comrades chuckle cheerfully, and I realize that Len and I have been invited to share an inside joke. The barriers are down. I translate, and when Len gives a hearty laugh, the comrades are delighted. The inspector puts his hand on my forearm and says: "Honored to know you both. Truly honored." His tone suddenly serious, he prompts: "Please translate for the Doctor."

Len smiles warmly: "Let's have a third round."

The two men decline apologetically, as the hour is getting late. The customs officer pulls a piece of paper from his pocket, saying, "This is my name and address. Please, I have a request. Write to me from America." He hands me the slip of paper, and, suddenly, with unexpected vehemence, he embraces me, then turns to Len and throws his arms around him.

Comrade Radek shyly kisses my hand, and parts from Len with a warm handshake. Len and I wave good-bye and watch the black limousine roll into the rainstorm. Then, huddled under my small umbrella, we begin the wet and windy trek to the bus station for Bratislava.

CHAPTER THIRTY-ONE

Nature Is Mourning

"Mom? Hello. It's me. I'm calling from Bratislava."

"Elli . . . Leah? How wonderful to hear your voice! How's Len?"

I'm fighting back tears. Mom's clear, energetic voice sounds so near.

"Leah? Are you there? I can't hear you."

"Mom, I called to tell you . . ." Tears jam my throat. Why does Mom call me Leah? I swallow hard. Finally I continue. "To tell you . . . we've completed the exhumation."

"You have?" Mom's voice turns hoarse. "You have?" There is a strange silence at the other end and I know Mother is weeping. We weep together, Mother in her home in Israel and I in my hotel room in Czechoslovakia—one heart, continents apart. Finally I clear my throat and ask: "Mom, did you know there was a porcelain jug in Grandfather's grave?"

"Yes . . ." She is struggling to regain her composure. "I remember. You see, my dear father, may his memory be a blessing, was a Levite. It's a traditional custom to bury Levites with a jug. The jug is the symbol of the tribe of Levi."

"And, Mom . . . did you know that Grandmother's dentures had several gold teeth in the upper row? Do you remember that?"

"How do you know?"

"Her dentures were in the grave."

"Oh, my God!" A muffled silence again, and then a pained, hoarse, barely audible voice reaches me: "I can't remember . . ." I can hear soft sobs at the other end, then, in a stifled voice, Mother whispers: "You actually *saw* the dentures?"

"Yes, Mom. We did the exhumation ourselves, Len and I. There was no *Hevra Kadisha*."

"The two of you?!" Her question ends in a shriek. "Oh my dear God!" After another long pause, Mom sobs into the phone: "Leah? Is Len there with you? Please tell him . . . tell Len, God bless him." Mother's voice trails off. "God bless him for what he's done . . . God bless you both."

"Mom, we'll see you soon. I'll call again, soon, to let you know our flight schedule, as soon as we've made the arrangements. Perhaps tomorrow."

"God bless you both . . ." I can hear Mom sobbing thousands of miles away, and I respond with a new round of weeping. Why did Mom call me Leah, my Hebrew name? Does she sense my deep identification with Leah, her mother, after whom she named me? Does she feel the mystical bond that was created by the intimate contact with her remains?

I must not allow myself to become submerged in these sentiments . . . I must move on. I have to make arrangements for our next moves. First, I place a call to Herr Handler, to inform him that the exhumation has been carried out.

"Well done!" Herr Handler exclaims when he hears the news. "Where are the caskets now?"

"They are stored with the Burial Commission in Samorin," I inform him. "We've made arrangements for the coffins to be shipped to the Austrian border on Wednesday morning. Can you arrange for us to be picked up at the border?" I inquire.

An hour later, Herr Handler phones to say that a hearse from Vienna will await us at the Austrian border at 9:00 a.m. on Wednesday, and will deliver us, together with the caskets, to the Vienna airport. The caskets will be stored with El Al Airlines until our flight to Israel on Thursday morning. "Your tickets will be waiting for you here at Atlastours, my office, at Wednesday noon. I'll see you then. Good luck."

Mr. Handler's businesslike correctness is reassuring. It is 10:20 p.m., 11:20 in Israel—too late to call Mother again.

"I hope it's not too late to visit Viola and Samira," I say to Len.

"Not at all," says Len. "They are expecting us. They undoubtedly are keen to hear all about the exhumation. I wouldn't worry about the hour."

We walk briskly through wet, dark streets to Viola's flat. Both women spring to their feet when we enter. They are eager to hear our news.

"What time did you finish the exhumation?" is Viola's first question.

"Why, about two."

"I knew it!" she exclaims. "I knew it! Samira, didn't I tell you?"

Samira smiles. "Yes, it was two o'clock in the afternoon."

I'm baffled. "What do you mean? What made you guess the exact time?"

Viola's eyes shine. "I did not guess; I *knew*."

"You see," Samira explains with uncharacteristic agitation, "at two o'clock the sky suddenly turned dark, and heavy raindrops began to fall. Mother said: 'They must've just finished the exhumation. The heavens are crying; a great *tzadik* was taken from the bosom of our land. Nature is mourning the loss of a righteous man.'"

Viola's eyes are bright with emotion. She says in a whisper: "It was no coincidence. The heavens turned dark and I heard thunder. I knew instantly. There are no coincidences."

There is silence in the room as Viola continues: "I knew Uncle Roth. He was a saintly man. I was about twelve when he died. All the children loved him, and attended his funeral; he was our friend. We all mourned him."

Viola's words have a profound effect on Len. I have never seen him so moved. In soft tones he begins to tell the tale of the bees, and the women listen, their eyes open wide with excitement. Viola whispers in awe: "This was another outcry. Nature's outcry against a violation. Nature's trauma. A *tzadik* has been taken from its bosom."

Len and I, even Viola and Samira, sit transfixed with the new revelation. Still unable to believe my ears, ultimately I break the spell by asking: "Viola, who spoke those words? The lifelong Communist or the Jew?"

Viola's sudden chuckle is laced with nostalgia: "The Communist with the Jewish heart."

CHAPTER THIRTY-TWO

Czechoslovakia Is Behind Us!

ON WEDNESDAY MORNING LEN AND I ARE SITTING IN THE HOTEL LOBBY, waiting anxiously for Tibor the hearse driver. At ten to seven, the short, stocky figure strides into the carpeted lobby of the Carlton with cocky brusqueness, his abrupt appearance startling us to our feet.

While Len helps Tibor arrange the suitcases in the cabin of the hearse, I peer through the smoked-glass window in the rear with bated breath. Ah, there they are; the silver-painted caskets, the names in large, glossy black letters clearly visible on each lid——LEAH on one, and SIMHA ZVI on the other. Thank God.

We are taking off. Tibor, Len, and I sit in the front seat of the hearse. As I look back I can see the Carlton disappear after a sharp turn in the road. Will the Carlton vanish from my inner world now that the dream has come full circle? Does a dream ever come full circle?

Tibor leans over and interrupts my thoughts with an unexpected question: "How do I get to the Austrian border?" he asks.

"You are asking *me*? Don't you know the road? Aren't you from around here?"

"Yes, madam. But I've never driven to the Austrian border. You must direct me."

This simply can't be happening. How, for goodness' sake, can I direct him? I must not panic. I must think . . . "Tibor, do you know the ramp that leads to the new bridge?"

"That I know."

"Good. Then get onto that ramp and cross the bridge. There will be signs to Vienna, and we'll follow them. That should be the road to the border."

I hope I'm right.

"Len, do you think there could be more than one road to Vienna? We have to be on the right road, at the right crossing, so as not to miss the hearse from Vienna."

"I don't know. There might. Why do you ask?"

"We must direct the driver. He doesn't know the way."

"What? Where is he from?"

"Samorin. But he has never driven to the border, he says."

What a relief it was to see the first road sign on the bridge: TO VIENNA. After a sharp right, we are on the way to Vienna. Was it only a week ago that we traveled this road in the opposite direction? A week? An eternity wrapped in a week. No one has invented an instrument to measure relative time. Clocks, calendars—how obsolete they really are, how inadequate. They tell nothing of a week such as this.

We reach the watchtower with the machine-gun-toting guards. As one of them approaches the hearse, Tibor, fidgeting in his seat, whispers between clenched teeth: "You talk to him, ma'am."

"I? Why wouldn't *you* talk to him?"

"I don't speak the language. These border guards, they're tough. You can explain everything to him, ma'am . . ."

"But I counted on you. I don't know Slovak anymore—not very well. You are from these parts, Tibor. I'm a stranger here."

The uniformed guard reaches the hearse and leans in through the open window. I have no choice: I quickly muster some words, and the guard nods. He reaches for the voluminous dossier of documents on my lap and returns to his post at a run. The wind rips at his green shirt as he talks on the telephone at some length. What is wrong? Why the lengthy talk? Now the younger guard gallops toward us, clutching the dossier in his hand. He shoves the dossier through the window and waves the driver on: "You may proceed."

Tibor visibly relaxes, and starts the motor. I open the orange flap of the dossier. Our passports are missing!

Meanwhile, Tibor is happily putting distance between himself and the guard post.

"Tibor, stop! Please pull back to the guard post. Our passports are gone."

Tibor continues to drive at full speed. "We can't go back!" he shouts in panic. "We can't go back. We can't provoke the guards. You never know what they'll think, what they'll do!"

"What's the matter?" Len asks.

"The passports are missing, and the driver is afraid to turn back. Stop the hearse! Let the hearse stay here. I'm returning on foot."

The young guard notices that the hearse has come to a stop. He approaches us at a run.

"Our passports!" I shout into the wind.

The young soldier stops dead in his tracks, and the wind carries his exclamation: "Jesus Maria!" Then he turns on his heels and races like a rabbit back to the post. Almost instantly, the young guard reemerges, galloping and waving the passports triumphantly in his right hand.

"Thank you very much!"

The young border guard salutes the departing hearse. I wave good-bye through the window, then shut it against the fierce wind.

A barrier blocks the highway: the border. My statement is rehearsed and ready in smooth Slovak for the approaching police officers. They ask no questions. They glance at the documents and signal toward the barrier. The barrier lifts. An elegant black funeral limousine passes under it and keeps rolling toward us.

"Darling, look! The hearse from Vienna! Things are working like a charm."

Like clockwork, the shiny limo from Vienna lines up behind the drab van, and two smartly uniformed attendants deftly transfer the caskets. Soon, we're ready to take off.

"Tibor, how much do I owe you?"

The Hungarian hearse driver pulls pencil and paper from his pocket and starts calculating. I am waiting on pins and needles while Tibor makes endless calculations on his scrap of paper. The Viennese attendants are in a hurry, and the border police are impatient. Traffic is piling up. But Tibor is still scribbling figures.

"Okay," he says finally, sweat coursing down his visage from under the visor of the blue cap. "Five hundred and forty crowns."

"How did you arrive at that figure? By my calculations it's two hundred and fifty, at most."

Tibor turns the piece of paper over on the other side, and starts his calculations anew.

"For God's sake, Tibor. Don't hold us up any longer. Let me help you out. Look: It's less than twenty kilometers from Samorin to Bratislava. Let's figure twenty. From Bratislava to the border, it's less than two. Let's say twenty-two altogether. It's eleven crowns per kilometer. Multiply twenty-two by eleven, and you get two hundred and forty-two."

The befuddled Hungarian hesitates.

I hand him three Czechoslovak banknotes. "Here's two hundred and fifty; it includes an extra tip for you."

But Tibor has not yet completed his calculations.

"Tibor, please take the money, and let us go."

The police officers approach the van to see what is holding up operations.

"Two hundred and fifty? That's highway robbery," one of them exclaims. "How can you take so much money from this lady for driving a van from Samorin to this border? It's a cat's leap!"

"He doesn't speak Slovak," I explain.

"What does he speak?"

"Hungarian."

The two Czechs look at each other and burst out laughing: "That explains it. Hungarian schools don't go above ten in arithmetic." It must be a standing Czech joke.

"Let's put him out of his misery," says the second officer. He takes the bills from my hand and gives them to the short, stocky Hungarian, still submerged in figures. "Here," he says in Hungarian. "Take these and go. You're a lucky man; this lady is very generous."

"*Dobry den!*" The officers salute me, and one of them gives Tibor a patronizing tap on the shoulder.

Tibor, still deep in thought, walks to his van, carrying the bills in his hand with care.

I run to the limousine, hop in next to Len in the backseat, and the driver starts the engine. Within seconds we cross the border into Austria. Czechoslovakia is behind us!

CHAPTER THIRTY-THREE

Austrian Sensitivity

I SIGH IN FERVENT PRAYER. CZECHOSLOVAKIA IS BEHIND US. MY TREPIDATION IS over. The threat of arrest . . . of a long prison term . . . is over!

"*Gottesdank!*" the driver cries in German. "No more hurdles from here on."

One of the attendants explains: "First of all, we'll check in the caskets at Schwechat at Austrian Airlines for tomorrow's flight. It will not take more than five minutes. We'll be in Vienna in no time!"

It is ten o'clock when we pull into the freight zone at the airport. The attendants advise us to wait in the hearse while they make arrangements for the storage of the coffins. Five minutes, at most.

Fifteen minutes pass, and no attendants. At ten-thirty Len suggests that I go to investigate. The huge depot seems deserted. The attendants are nowhere. I have no choice but to walk back to the hearse and rejoin Len, waiting.

At eleven I unwrap our sandwiches.

"Lunch in a hearse?" Len says with a spark of mischief in his eye. Our tension is broken.

At eleven thirty-five several men emerge from the depot. I get out of the hearse to meet them.

"There's big trouble," the younger attendant declares. "The bodies have to be re-crated. The airline will not ship coffins."

"What? But why? Where do we get the crates?"

"You have to order crates in Vienna, at a shipping company, and they will do the re-crating."

"Oh no, no. Out of the question. Those caskets won't be opened. What else can be done?"

Rapid consultation in German produces no solution. Len calls from the hearse: "What's going on? What's all the fuss?" His face falls when he hears the story.

"How on earth can all that be accomplished today even if we would agree?"

"Today's out. I don't think all that could be accomplished even tomorrow. And the day after tomorrow is Friday. We'd have to spend the weekend in Vienna!"

Now the senior attendant turns to me: "Another big trouble. Big. The Austrian customs don't accept the Czechoslovak customs certification. They want to reinspect. We have to return to the border for customs inspection."

My heart starts flapping like a dying fish in a cooking pot.

"Hey, no hurdles," I say. "Isn't that what you promised?" I snatch the papers from the attendant's hand. "Which one of you gentlemen is the customs officer?"

The attendant points at a bulky body in a red-striped shirt.

"Look . . ."—my voice is shaking—"the Czech customs sealed the coffins at the cemetery, hermetically soldering them in zinc. The document says 'For all international agencies.' That's not good enough for you? Do you think the Czechs would allow contraband goods to leave their country? What you ask is not humanly possible."

"*Ja, ja*," the funeral attendant explains to me. "It's not up to him. It's the border police. It's up to them."

Len asks no questions. His face reflects the helpless despair he reads on mine. "May I suggest that you go to the shipping company right away, and buy the crates." The attendant is trying to be helpful. "Tomorrow morning, when you return to the border, take the crates along, and when they open the coffins for inspection, the bones can be transferred into the crates right there. You would be done by noon, at the latest."

"These caskets will not be opened. They are the sacred remains of my grandparents, and they will not be tampered with by anyone! We have a flight scheduled for tomorrow morning at eight, and the caskets are expected with that flight at Ben-Gurion Airport, at eleven a.m. An entire funeral party is awaiting us at the airport—a hearse with attendants, mourners, all the family of the deceased, including my ninety-year-old mother. What do you expect me to do?"

I'm raising my voice, and the men listen in stunned silence. Then the customs officer mumbles something to the others, and they all disappear into the building.

Ten minutes later the attendants return with a secretive smile.

"The flight is on for tomorrow morning," the older one announces enigmatically.

"What do you mean? What's happened?"

The younger one starts the engine and the hearse is whizzing across the freight yard toward the depot.

"*Alles ist erledigt.* Everything's been taken care of. We are sending the coffins just as they are. No inspection. No re-crating. Everything's under control."

Two men in blue overalls come out of the depot, remove the caskets from the hearse, and place them on a cart. The men, the cart, and the caskets rapidly vanish into the enormous maw of the depot.

"What's happening? Where are they taking the caskets?"

The attendant mumbles something, and I repeat my question.

"*Keine Ahnung* . . . No idea," the attendant mutters. I hop out of the hearse and race after the cart.

In the warehouse the caskets are balanced on a forklift.

"Where are you putting those caskets?" I shout to the workmen above the deafening din of the warehouse.

"Onto the aircraft," one of them shouts back.

"What aircraft?"

"Alitalia."

"Alitalia?! Where to?"

"Rome."

"Rome??! Why Rome? Who gave you orders to put these on a flight to Rome?" I shout, beside myself. The workman shrugs his shoulders and continues to operate the forklift.

The funeral attendant catches up. "Do you know anything about this? The caskets are being shipped to Rome! Who gave this order?" The attendant hesitates, and I do not wait for his answer.

"Stop that crane!" I roar. "Take those caskets off that crane!"

"We can't. The flight is in thirty minutes."

"Stop! This shipment is not going to Rome! This is my shipment. And I am not permitting you to put it on this flight!"

The forklift stops in midair. "I'm sorry, but I am answerable to my foreman," the worker shouts his reply.

"Who's your foreman? I'll talk to him."

"I work for Schencker's. Upstairs." He points toward the staircase.

"Hold that forklift!"

I fly toward the staircase. On the first floor I barge through a door marked SCHENCKER SHIPMENTS, startling a young fat clerk on the phone. He quickly covers the receiver with one hand and asks: "What can I do for you?"

"I want you to stop the shipment of the caskets immediately! They are not supposed to go to Rome!"

The frightened young clerk hurriedly whispers into the telephone, and hangs up. He turns to me with a courteous gesture and asks in a conciliatory tone: "Madam, am I to understand that you do *not* want to ship the coffins by Alitalia to Rome? We have just received instructions from Herr Handler. But if you want to alter them, *bitte*, I will take care of it immediately."

He makes several quick calls. Then he turns to me again with a flourish of courtesy. "It's done. The Rome shipment is canceled. The coffins are scheduled for shipment tomorrow, Austrian Airlines, flight 206, to Tel Aviv."

"Thank you," I say. "But I need some proof of shipment. Please give me a receipt of some sort—something by which I can identify the shipment."

"This is the cargo number. You can claim the cargo with this number," says the clerk, scribbling a number on a piece of paper.

"Thank you." I snatch the note and dash out of the office, the hearse attendants in tow. We race toward the hearse where Len impatiently fidgets in the backseat.

"Everything's a go. Next stop, Vienna," I blurt out breathlessly. "We must reach Atlastours before two, to pick up our tickets and settle our account with Mr. Handler."

"We'll never make it. It's one twenty-five now."

I turn to the attendants: "Would you please take us to the passenger terminal? We'll take a taxi from there."

"We'll do better than that," the older attendant says with a wink. "We'll drive you to Vienna, straight to Atlastours. You'll make it before two."

The hearse moves at breakneck speed, cutting corners, whizzing through narrow alleys, and raising eyebrows on busy Vienna streets. It comes to a dead stop on the corner of Weihburgstrasse at one fifty-two.

Herr Handler is in his office. A shocking bit of news awaits us. He switched our flight to Israel from 8:00 a.m. tomorrow to 3:00 p.m. today!

"But why?" My question is a cry of despair. "I have just made sure the caskets will be shipped tomorrow morning, with our flight!"

"That was a mistake. That's an Austrian Airlines flight, the airline that demanded re-crating. Austrian tact. They do not want to shock their passengers with an accidental glimpse of coffins being lifted in and out of the aircraft. That's why I shifted the shipment to Alitalia, via Rome to Tel Aviv. Alitalia regularly flies Catholics for burial in Rome. Its passengers are used to the sight of coffins en route. When you kicked up a fuss over shipping the coffins via Rome, I had no choice but to switch to El Al, the Israeli airline. But El Al does not fly tomorrow morning. The only possibility is the afternoon flight, today." Herr Handler looks worn.

"Herr Handler, I'm so sorry . . . I did not know the reason behind the Rome shipment. I thought it was a misunderstanding. I was afraid that my grandparents' bones would end up in Rome instead of Jerusalem. There is a slight difference between the two, you'd agree." I manage a wan smile.

"It's too late to make the switch," Herr Handler explains with a sigh.

"But the afternoon flight gets us to Israel too late in the day for burial. You see, arrangements have been made with the burial society to drive the caskets straight from the airport to Jerusalem for the funeral. I notified my brother of the time of our arrival tomorrow noon. My brother, who flew to Israel from New York with his family for the funeral, must have by now alerted all the family members, all the descendants of my grandparents living in

Israel, to await the arrival of the caskets at Ben-Gurion Airport tomorrow noon."

"We can call the burial society in Jerusalem, right now," says Herr Handler. "They will be able to handle the switch. They are used to emergencies. After all, every funeral is an emergency according to Orthodox law. They will notify the family as well, if you give them your mother's phone number. They have a couple of hours at their disposal . . ."

"But, Herr Handler, we would be arriving in the evening. You can't have a funeral at night."

"I think, yes. I think, according to Jewish custom, the dead must be buried immediately, sometimes at night. We'll check with the Jerusalem funeral society." Herr Handler reaches for the telephone, and a few seconds later hands me the receiver.

"Long distance is on the line. Please give the Jerusalem funeral society's number to the operator."

The connection to Jerusalem is crystal clear, and I'm able to understand the funeral director's rapid Hebrew without difficulty.

"No problem," he assures me. "The funeral van will be at Ben-Gurion at 6:30 p.m., and our people will take care of all official business at the depot. Once the caskets are cleared, the van will drive to the passenger terminal and wait for all the mourners so that they can follow in their cars. The procession will head for Har Hamenuhot, the Hill of Repose Cemetery in Jerusalem, and the funeral will take place right then."

I ask the funeral director to contact my mother, and he readily consents to inform her of the switch. He assures me that all will be in order.

I sigh with relief. Len, who stands next to me and overhears the conversation, goes into "active mode."

"Good," he cries. "Let me call for a taxi. We must leave for the airport at once."

"Len, our Israeli passports! They are at the Goldene Spinne."

"Oh my God!"

Herr Handler phones for a taxi.

"A detour to the Goldene Spinne will be cutting it fine, but a clever driver can make it on time. I will give directions to the driver when the taxi gets here."

"Thank you, Herr Handler—you have been simply wonderful. By the way, how did you get the Austrian customs to relent?"

"It wasn't easy. I'm still having abdominal pains." He smiles and hands Len our tickets, then picks up one of our suitcases to help carry them to the street.

A car is honking on the street. The taxi. Mr. Handler gives the driver instructions for shortcuts to the Hotel Goldene Spinne and from there to Schwechat, the airport.

Herr Handler plants a fatherly kiss on my cheek. "Good luck. Let me know how it all goes in Jerusalem."

"*Vielen Dank!*"

The driver turns on the ignition, and Len gives my hand an enthusiastic squeeze. "We are on our way, darling. We are on our way!"

At the Goldene Spinne, Herr Johann welcomes me with effusive joy and a barrage of questions about our trip to Czechoslovakia. I blurt out: "*Herr Johann, um Gottes Willen!* We are in a great hurry. I need our Israeli passports, fast. We're on our way to the airport!"

"Passports? What passports? I know nothing of your passports."

"Herr Johann, you yourself put them in the safe a week ago."

Herr Johann cannot remember.

"Please," I implore. "Herr Johann, we are in a terrible hurry. I can show you where you put them in the safe."

The clerk fumbles among the keys, then waddles downstairs right behind me. The manila envelope with our Israeli passports is not in the safe.

"Perhaps Herr Bloch, the manager, put them in the other safe in the other office."

"And where is Herr Bloch?" Herr Johann never knew where Herr Bloch was when not at the hotel. He could be in many different places. Perhaps he was at the other office.

"Herr Johann, I beg of you—try to remember where he could be now. Perhaps you can reach him."

"Frau Jackson, it is not possible for me to do that. I never call him except in an emergency."

"But surely this is an emergency! We cannot travel to Israel without our Israeli passports."

Herr Johann turns the pages of his notebook, then speaks into the large mouthpiece of the antediluvian telephone. After a brief conversation, he says, "You see, Frau Jackson, Herr Bloch, my boss, is a very kind man. He has the passports in the safe in his other office, and he's bringing them right over in a taxi. You're very fortunate."

"When will he get here?"

"Oh, about forty or forty-five minutes."

"Herr Johann," I cry, "our plane is leaving at three-thirty. That's less than an hour! We can't wait here until Herr Bloch arrives."

A thought flashes through my mind. "Herr Johann, listen carefully: Please ask Herr Bloch to bring the passports straight to the airport, to the El Al counter, as soon as he can get there. Will you do that, please?"

I whip out a piece of paper and jot down the information.

"*Auf Wiedersehen,* Herr Johann. *Danke vielmals.* Our heartfelt greetings to Herr Bloch."

Len's face lights up when I approach the taxi. The driver competently guides the taxi through traffic to the open highway. At 3:00 p.m. it comes to a stop in front of the departure building at the Vienna airport.

Len hops out, and I untangle his coat's belt buckle from the door latch of the taxi while he pays the driver. Neck and neck we race through the sliding doors of the terminal. Len races ahead to the El Al counter and I navigate the luggage cart through pedestrian traffic. When I reach him, Len brandishes our Israeli passports: Mr. Bloch has delivered them. And he puts on his you-see-all's-well face.

Once again, I am happy to let him have the last word.

CHAPTER THIRTY-FOUR

Where Are the Coffins?

THE STARTLED EL AL STEWARD HURRIEDLY PICKS UP THE TELEPHONE TO INFORM the gate of our arrival as I shove our passports and the note with the cargo number under his nose.

"Hurry. Gate 6. Go directly to the boarding gate."

"Please check that this cargo is aboard. We can't board until then. We can't fly without this cargo."

"There's no time. You must board immediately."

I spot an El Al officer and run up to him to explain my problem. He echoes the steward's words: "There's no time. You must board immediately."

"I'm not boarding until the coffins have been checked out. I must know if they are aboard the plane!" I shout in despair.

The El Al officer speaks into his transmitter, and within seconds comes the answer: "The coffins are not on the flight."

Len and I look at each other in disbelief.

"What do you mean?" Len asks. "Where are they?"

"I am not boarding until the coffins are found!" I shout.

"Madam," the steward pleads. "You're holding up the flight."

"I'm sorry," I cry. "I cannot leave without the coffins."

"Don't you understand?" Len is indignant. "We are not leaving without the coffins."

The officer telephones the shipping company. His face is somber as he announces: "The coffins are in Tel Aviv."

"In Tel Aviv? How is that possible? We left them at the depot this morning, here at Schwechat. How can they be in Tel Aviv? They were to be put on this flight. It's imperative that we arrive together."

"This must be a mistake," Len says. "When were they shipped?"

"An hour ago a cargo plane left for Tel Aviv. They were put on that plane," the officer says with a sigh.

"I must know for sure. I must know where the coffins are before I board the plane," I declare for the fifth time.

The El Al officer dials Ben-Gurion Airport in Tel Aviv. A few minutes later, he says, "Madam, Ben-Gurion just confirmed it. The coffins are there. Someone made a mistake and put the coffins on the cargo plane. I'm sorry, madam."

"Your boarding passes, please." The voice of the steward at Gate 6 reaches me through a haze.

I walk up the ramp, board the plane, and slip into my seat like an automaton. The pilot's voice vaguely touches the perimeter of fatigue that envelops my senses. Len holds my hand. His clasp is warm and reassuring, and I grip his hand as one grips a lifeline out of an abyss, the promise of hope. The promise that everything will be okay: that the caskets will be found . . . that my family will be at the airport . . . that the undertakers from Jerusalem will arrive on time . . . and that the funeral will take place as I had hoped.

The sun breaks through the clouds, and, as the plane rises above them, they frame the frothy, shimmering sea below. I can feel the golden glow of sunshine as it sifts through the fog, as it thins the clouds and sets them adrift, far into the distance.

———— ⋅ ✦ ⋅ ————

There on the dawning horizon the hazy outline of a statue precipitates out of the fog.

"The Statue of Liberty!"

A cheer rings out among the ranks of refugees crowding the rails. The sound ripples the rays of the rising sun amid the fog. I wish I knew the American anthem. Instead, the Israeli anthem reverberates in my mind. It sings of hope—and home—as Lady Liberty comes closer and closer: "Our hope is not lost—to return to the Land of our fathers, the Land of Zion and Jerusalem . . ."

———— • ————

Len's voice reaches me: "Wake up, darling, we've arrived. I'm glad you had a nice, long nap. You slept through the entire journey."

"I have? I was very tired. . . . Look, Len, it's the Tel Aviv coastline!"

"I know," Len says with a smile. "What did you expect?"

The coastline is studded with a thousand lights, and white sails bob in the dark waves. The aircraft shudders with the impact, and soon, Len is reaching for the hand luggage in the overhead bin. "It has been a long journey. It seems as if we were away for ages," he says with a sigh.

"Yes, it does . . . I believe it *was* ages."

"Why so solemn?" Len asks, as we approach the aircraft exit.

"I'm just concerned about the coffins. I hope they will be found. I hope the funeral van will come on time. I hope my family will be there . . . I hope . . ."

We reach the steep metal steps and descend, one behind the other. We pile into the airbus, and it starts with a sudden lurch. Then it swings around to deposit its human cargo at the passenger terminal.

CHAPTER THIRTY-FIVE

Homecoming

THE AIR, HUMID AND WARM, EMBRACES US LIKE AMNIOTIC FLUID. IT SURGES about us, vital and pulsating, filling the vacuum of the softly descending dusk.

Mother and the others are there, beyond the railing, waving and calling out words of welcome.

Len and I press ahead through the nothing to declare column, toward the exit and the dense hustle and bustle of Ben-Gurion Airport. The welcoming group begins to surge forward. But then, as if on cue, Mother separates from the crowd, advancing toward us, and all the others come to a standstill like an ebbing ocean pushing forward a single object from its midst. Mother's stooped figure, her entire being, sparkles with anticipation as she advances with frail steps, fragile arms half-raised in welcome.

I rush into her open arms, and we float in a silent embrace.

"Welcome. Welcome," she whispers hoarsely. At long last.

I'm unable to utter a sound.

Mother reaches out to Len and he envelops her delicate body in his embrace.

"Thank you for all you have done, Len. May God bless you." Her voice breaks. Len bends down to kiss her cheek, and his eyes are brimming with tears.

The tide surges forward now and closes in about us. Most of my family is here—my brother, Bubi (Simha Zvi), his wife and three children, my cousins, their spouses, their children and grandchildren—three generations, welcoming the ancestors on their return from exile. Of the seven children in her family, Mother alone has lived to witness this heartrending event. Out of the seven, four perished in Auschwitz and two have died since. Six of eight surviving grandchildren and two of thirteen great-grandchildren are present to greet the ancestral remains.

The family engulfs us with cries of welcome, a volley of questions. The questions are insistent, eager, impatient. Len and I answer, and our responses begin to sound like a chant, a rhythmic, tribal affirmation.

"Yes, we did accomplish the exhumation. No, there was no *Hevra Kadisha*. Yes, the coffins are sealed. No, there were no tombstones. Yes, the bones were intact. No, neither tombstone was there. Yes, we are certain that we brought the right bones. No, there was no danger. Yes, the funeral will be held tonight. Yes, the coffins are here. No, I was not arrested. Yes, the funeral van will be here soon. Yes, the funeral . . ."

The funeral van pulls up to the curb. I fumble in my handbag, and find the note with the cargo number. Len hands the note to one of the funeral attendants, and the van takes off in the direction of the freight yard to fetch the coffins.

The human tide closes in again, and the questions and answers resume a ritualistic incantation: Yes—Yes—No—No—Yes—Yes . . .

The funeral van returns and a sudden hush falls on the crowd. The funeral director, dressed in a black caftan and a black hat with a wide brim, flings open the rear doors, and there, from the dark interior of the van, two small, silver-painted caskets confront the stunned audience. The letters on one of the caskets, in large, glossy black, read LEAH, and, on the other, SIMHA ZVI.

The funeral director calls for ten men of those present, all relatives, to form a quorum for prayer. The men in the crowd respond, immediately clustering around the open door of the van. The funeral director hands out copies of the *Book of Psalms*, and my brother leads the group in reciting the ancient Jewish hymns.

The two attendants' voices rise in a chant, and the quorum of mourners joins in the haunting sounds of the age-old melody. The night thickens and the melody filters through the dark, warm, humid breeze, flapping the Israeli flag at the entrance of the terminal building. The melody seeps through the sounds of traffic—taxis and buses, passenger cars and bicycles—it percolates through the confusion of people passing in all directions, welcoming all arrivals.

Now the doors of the van close, and the entire company files into cars. The cars line up behind the funeral van, a small caravan, and follow it out of the airport, onto the open highway.

Mom, Len, and I sit in our Fiat, driven by Bubi. I hold Mother's hand, and our silence is broken only by an occasional sigh bursting from her lips.

There is so much to say. Only silence could capture all there is to say.

Darkness lurks in the forests we are passing as the road winds its way upward to Jerusalem. The hills of Jerusalem loom dark against the pale moonlight. The road curves higher and higher. Chill air rushes in through the open car window, and I shiver. As Len leans over to roll up the window, Mother grasps his hand. Len lifts the thin, bony hand and raises it to his lips. Mother's sudden sharp intake of breath is a sob.

Bubi drives fast, competently, handling the curves with ease. The last sharp turn brings the car onto the path that leads to the cemetery, the Hill of Repose. Here, the lights of the highway vanish, and the car makes its upward climb in total darkness. Near the top of the hill the funeral van stands still, waiting for the other cars to catch up. Bubi slows the car and the van moves again, leading the way upward on the flank of the hill, rising ever higher among tombs of bleached rock glimmering in the moonlight.

The moon is fixed in the center of the firmament, pale and stark, among a thousand stars. There is not even a hint of haze; the stars glisten with awesome immediacy. The sudden, unexpected proximity of the brilliant sky seems to reveal a deep secret. Is it the message of immortality?

The van stops on top of the hill, at the foot of a flight of stairs carved out of pink Jerusalem rock. The caravan of cars, a ribbed, graceless snake, comes to a standstill.

The mourners get out of their cars and begin the slow ascent toward the stairs. There, two members of the funeral society, black shadows in the moonlight, each carrying a casket on his shoulder, move skyward on the steep stone steps.

I take Mother's arm and follow right behind the casket bearers, and the others follow, up the steep stone stairs. Mother leans on my arm, and we walk slowly, step by step, toward the glittering sky. Mother's arm, thin and light, rests on mine with a steady grip until we reach a square terrace overlooking a dark abyss—the Jerusalem forest far below.

In the glow of the moon two holes yawn darkly. Next to each dark hole, an open casket reveals a white shrouded shape. When did the undertakers manage to open the sealed caskets? All seems to have been accomplished with an eerie expertise, by hands practiced at the business of death.

The cluster of mourners, dark silhouettes with bowed heads, begins to murmur another hymn while a savage night wind below shrieks with untamed vehemence. The tall pines shudder as two black figures lift a white shape out of the first casket and hoist it into the dark hole. The chant rises into a wail, as clumps of earth tumble like an avalanche, covering the gaping mouth of the earth. The chant grows louder, and the second shape is hoisted into the second hole. Black clods tumble and roll like molten lava, covering the fragile contents of the graves.

There is no outcry of earth or nature, no attack of wild bees, no violent storm protesting the arrival of the returning exiles. There is only the soft, silent welcoming embrace of the ancient homeland. The mournful, sonorous sounds of the *Kaddish,* the ancient affirmation of holiness in the presence of death, seems to take wing on the gusty breeze.

I raised you from your graves and brought you to the Land of your fathers ... the Land of Israel ... So sayeth the Lord: Do not weep, Rachel, your deeds are rewarded ... and they shall return ... your children shall return to their Land ...

Am I biblical Leah, a link in the chain of prophecy? Am I the sister of Rachel, bringing the exiles from distant parts of the globe to the Land of their Fathers, the Land of Israel, to quiet my sister Rachel's weeping ... to dry her tears?

I draw my mother's trembling body into my arms as the chant rises and swirls around us, melting our bodies into one, our embrace absorbing our bodies' rhythmic tremor.

Now my brother's voice is heard, delivering the eulogy. Simha Zvi, our grandfather's namesake, his eulogy is not a farewell; it's a greeting. His words are words of welcome, an invocation. His deep voice echoes in the night wind like a melody, a symphony of gratitude. This is not a funeral but a homecoming ... a celebration of return.

And they shall return ... your children shall return to their Land.

Suddenly, strangely, I am at peace.

I see my brother's imposing figure surrounded by his family. I see his wife and his sons, tall, skinny boys; his daughter, a gangly young girl with braids. I see Mother, stooped and frail yet indomitable in spirit. I see Len, his hair ruffled in the wind, his eyes aflame with the sense of mission accomplished. I see other members of the family, my cousins and their spouses and their children, their figures etched against the luminous firmament—children born and raised under this blessed starry sky, strong and confident . . . the new generation unmarred by the past.

But most of all, I see Mom, the initiator of this magnificent home-coming, tall but stooped, and wrapped in an aura of humble thanks-giving, the powerful night wind of Jerusalem swirling about her frail figure.

I am at peace. The world seems diminutive and safe. It stretches securely, studded with tiny dots of light in the distance. The pain, the uncertainty, the hopelessness—all belong to the past. Auschwitz recedes into another dimension.

My eyes scan the horizon with new knowledge. I hear the ancient chant, and it is mournful no more. It is a glorious anthem of promise and hope. A dark veil lifts from my soul: I am free at last.

The stars hang low and brilliant, welcoming the chant as it dances on the wings of the night wind toward the sparkling sky . . .

We are home.

EPILOGUE

TWENTY-EIGHT YEARS, NEARLY THREE DECADES, HAVE PASSED SINCE THAT remarkable night on the windswept hill in Jerusalem. Much has happened in these twenty-eight years.

Mother was united with her beloved parents seven years after their arrival in Jerusalem, and was placed in the earth beside her mother on the Hill of Repose. Four white monuments now rest on a secluded terrace high above Jerusalem. A white marble slab spans the gap between the two central tombs, the tombs of my grandfather and grandmother. On this slab are engraved the names of their children—Mom's siblings and their families—who do not have graves. They rose as smoke from the chimneys of Auschwitz.

This is their gravesite. This is their monument.

Father's name and a short legend are inscribed on Mom's gravestone. His eternal resting place is somewhere in a nameless mass grave in Germany, in another infamous death camp called Bergen-Belsen. Mother's tombstone in Jerusalem is his monument.

The morning before Len and I left for our incredible mission to retrieve my ancestors' remains from the rising waters of the Danube in Czechoslovakia, my first grandchild was born. The blue-eyed, golden-haired infant is a married woman now, a practicing lawyer in Jerusalem, and the mother of my first, Israeli-born, great-granddaughter, a brilliant blossom of a new generation.

During the intervening years my brother and his children made their homes in Israel. All of them—his young skinny boys and his little daughter, the gangly young girl with braids—are now accomplished professionals and parents of large families born in Israel.

And yet, I have not severed my bonds with the United States.

During the first two decades I continued to teach my classes at Lehman College of the City University of New York, commuting between the two worlds. Even after officially retiring, I have kept returning to teach during summer sessions, maintaining contact with old friends, colleagues, and family members on the western side of the Atlantic.

Most of all, I have been fortunate during these trips to America to participate in the lives of my two children who live there, watching their children grow and deriving great pleasure from their accomplishments.

During these years my son and daughter have also purchased homes in Jerusalem and made frequent visits to Israel with their families. For them, together with my brother's children and grandchildren, and for all other descendants, the four white monuments personify ancestral roots in the ancient Land of the Jews. The four white monuments serve as a mystical, magnetic presence high above Jerusalem.

Each time I approach the secluded terrace on the Hill of Repose, my heart fills with gratitude. Little did I know twenty-eight years ago that Mother's "bizarre" request would lead to a historical milestone, a tangible reality in all of our lives.

ABOUT THE AUTHOR

Ms. Bitton-Jackson was born Livia Elvira Friedmann, better known as "Elli," on February 28, 1931, in Samorin (Somorja in Hungarian), a small town in Czechoslovakia. She spent her childhood there with her parents and her older brother Bubi, at the foot of the Carpathian Mountains, one kilometer from the Danube River.

Hungarian troops occupied her region in 1938. In a way, this was a "lucky" turn of events, as Hitler did not catch up to the Hungarian Jews until 1944, when Elli was thirteen years old, and the war was already drawing to a close. But that did not mean that they were not persecuted. On March 25, 1944, schooling for Jewish children was terminated, without any explanation. Jews were forced to wear yellow stars, and matters steadily worsened. Jews were not allowed to talk, greet, or look at gentiles on the street, rendering many friends strangers overnight. Then all the Jews of Somorja were deported to Nagymagyar, another town where a ghetto was created for the Jews of her area.

Ms. Bitton-Jackson has written numerous works, including autobiographical accounts of her experiences, for both adults and young readers. Her adult publications include *Elli: Coming of Age in the Holocaust* and *Madonna or Courtesan?: The Jewish Woman in Christian Literature*. Her award-winning titles for young readers, which have become classics of the genre, include *I Have Lived a Thousand Years: Growing Up in the Holocaust*, *My Bridges of Hope: Searching for Life and Love After Auschwitz,* and *Hello, America: A Refugee's Journey from Auschwitz to the New World*.

ABOUT THE AUTHOR

For more than thirty years Ms. Bitton-Jackson has written a column on women in Jewish history for the New York weekly, *The Jewish Press*. Her doctoral dissertation, *Zionism in Hungary,* was published by Herzl Press. She has also written numerous monographs and chapters in other books.